CONTEMPORARY MAINSTREAM RELIGION

In memory of

MICHAEL DALLING

(1940-1992)

Whose fieldwork forms the basis of Chapter 4
but who did not live to see his findings in print

Contemporary Mainstream Religion

Studies from Humberside and Lincolnshire

Edited by
PETER G. FORSTER
Department of Sociology and Anthropology
University of Hull

Avebury

Aldershot · Brookfield USA · Hong Kong · Singapore · Sydney

BR
763
.H86
C66
1995

Published by
Avebury
Ashgate Publishing Limited
Gower House
Croft Road
Aldershot
Hants GU11 3HR
England

Ashgate Publishing Company
Old Post Road
Brookfield
Vermont 05036
USA

British Library Cataloguing in Publication Data

Contemporary Mainstream Religion: Studies
from Humberside and Lincolnshire
I. Forster, Peter G.
274.10825

ISBN 1-85628-919-2

Library of Congress Cataloging-in-Publication Data

Contemporary mainstream religion: Studies from Humberside and
    Lincolnshire / edited by Peter G. Forster.
        p.   cm.
    Includes index.
    ISBN 1-85628-919-2: £30.00 ($51.95)
    1. Christianity--England--Humberside. 2. Christianity--England-
    -Lincolnshire. 3. Humberside (England)--Church history--20th
    century. 4. Lincolnshire (England)--Church history--20th century.
    I. Forster, Peter G. (Peter Glover), 1944-   .
      BR763.H86C66   1995
      306.6'09425'3--dc20   94-37971
                                                                        CIP
Printed and bound by Athenæum Press Ltd.,
Gateshead, Tyne & Wear.

Contents

List of tables

Chapter 4

Chapter 5

List of contributors

Peter G. Forster is Senior Lecturer in the Department of Sociology and Anthropology of the University of Hull. His main publications include *The Esperanto Movement* (1982), *Church and People on Longhill Estate* (1989), *T. Cullen Young: Missionary and Anthropologist* (1989) and (edited with Sam Maghimbi) *The Tanzanian Peasantry: Economy in Crisis* (1992). (He is not to be confused with the Rev Dr Peter R. Forster, Vicar of Beverley Minster).

Roy Carr-Hill is Senior Research Fellow in the Department of Health Economics, University of York. His main publications include (with N.H. Stern) *Crime, the Police and Criminal Statistics* (1979); *Primary Education in Tanzania* (1984), (ed. with A. Bhat); *Britain's Black Population* (1988); (with S. McIver and P. Dixon) *The NHS and its Customers* (1989); *Social Conditions in Sub-Saharan Africa* (1990); (with G. Dalley) *Pathways to Quality* (1991); (with K. King) *International Aid to Basic Education* (1992); (with C. Pritchard) *Women's Social Standing* (1992); *Cultural Conditionality on Aid to Basic Education* (1993); and *The State and Teachers: A Research Project on Tanzania* (1994).

The late **Michael Dalling** graduated in Sociology and Social Anthropology at the University of Hull in 1988. At the time of his death in 1992, he was just completing work on a PhD thesis on farmers' response to agricultural change in north Lincolnshire. He has contributed to *Anthropology in Action*. It is hoped to publish posthumously some articles based on his PhD work.

Raymond Francis is Lecturer in the Department of Sociology and Anthropology of the University of Hull. He has edited (with Valdo Pons) *Urban Social Research: Problems and Prospects* (1983) and has contributed chapters to *Introduction to Social Research* (edited by Valdo Pons, 1988, 2nd ed. 1992).

Martin Shaw is Professor of Political and International Sociology in the Department of Sociology and Anthropology of the University of Hull, where he is currently Head of Department. His main publications include *Marxism versus Sociology: A Guide to Reading* (1974); *Marxism and Social Science: The Roots of Social Knowledge* (1975); (ed.) *War, State and Society* (1984); (ed.) *Marxist Sociology Revisited: Critical Assessments* (1985); (ed. with Colin Creighton) *The Sociology of War and Peace* (1987); *Dialectics of War* (1988); *Post-Military Society* (1991); and (ed. with M. Banks) *State and Society in International Relations* (1991).

Christine Spencer graduated from the Department of Sociology of the University of Liverpool in 1981. She completed her MPhil thesis in the Department of Sociology and Anthropology of the University of Hull in 1990.

Adrian Worsfold obtained the tripartite degree in Economics, Politics and Sociology of the University of Hull in 1981. He completed his PhD from the Department of Sociology and Anthropology in 1989. He has contributed articles to *Faith and Freedom*.

Acknowledgements

All the studies in this collection are based upon empirical research. Accordingly the investigators have taken up the time of numerous clergy, churchpeople and others when gathering the relevant information. The assistance of all who cooperated with the investigators is hereby gratefully acknowledge.

I am grateful for financial support provided by the University Research Support Fund, and by the Department of Sociology and Anthropology of the University of Hull, for preparation of the text and updating of fieldwork. I am also grateful to Stella Rhind who typed the final version.

Chapter 1 (in an earlier version) appeared in the *Sociological Review*, 3 (1989), pp. 474-504. I am grateful to Routledge for permission to reproduce the material in the present volume. I am also grateful to MARC Europe, now the Christian Research Association, for permission to reproduce material in Tables 1, 2 and 3 from the *UK Christian Handbook* 1989/90 and 1992/3 (P. Brierley [1988] and P. Brierley and D. Longley [1991]); and material in Tables 6 and 7 from *Prospects for the Nineties* (P. Brierley [1991]). Table 4 is an adaptation of figures presented in *Values and Social Change in*

Britain, by M. Abrams, D. Gerard and N. Timms; I am grateful to Macmillan for permission to reproduce this material.

Introduction

Peter G. Forster

This is a collection of studies of mainstream Christianity, that is, of the long-established Christian churches rather than of the smaller sects or cults, whether of recent or much older origin.

It is important that such material should be made available, as there is much support for the view that empirical research concerning mainstream Christianity in England has been neglected by sociologists of religion. Turner (1983, pp. 3-5) has commented that 'the trend towards the sociology of cults has now gone so far that mainstream Christianity has to some extent been neglected'. Similarly, Wallis and Bruce have remarked that 'apart from work on British and Irish Catholicism, the mainstream churches have been neglected in recent time' (1989, p. 511). Moreover Davie (1990, p. 396) has observed as follows:

> We have considerable - and increasing - evidence about small pieces of the religious jigsaw in this country, and not least about its more exotic edges; in contrast the picture in the middle remains alarmingly blurred. We discover that there is very little knowledge

indeed about the beliefs of ordinary British people and the significance of these beliefs in or for everyday life.

There have been discussions of the overall religious scene in England, Britain, the United Kingdom, Europe or the West (e.g. Wilson, 1966; Martin, 1967; MacIntyre, 1967; Forster, 1972; Social Surveys, 1964; Davie, 1990); but in all cases such research has been based on historical and statistical materials, and has not involved empirical study of religion in relation to local situations. Furthermore, some important items in the literature on mainstream Christianity are twenty to twenty-five years old, and there is considerable evidence of change in the position of mainstream Christianity in England since the late sixties and early seventies.

Much of the discussion in the recent past has been concerned with the process of 'secularization'. Wilson sees religious thinking and practices and the institutionalization and organization of these patterns of thought and action as having lost influence in Western societies generally. He acknowledges that the changes are uneven and that they occur in different ways in different societies (Wilson, 1966). Martin has been more cautious in the use of the concept of secularization, and he has stressed that important elements of 'religiosity' remain, and that the process is not necessarily irreversible (Martin, 1965; 1967, esp. Ch. 2). However, Wilson has also accepted that sectarian forms of religion can remain when the mainstream churches' influence upon society is on the wane (Wilson, 1966, p. 233). It may be the case then that although there remains important differences between the approaches of Martin and Wilson, both of them agree to a greater or lesser extent that religion can persist but that it will be pushed towards the periphery. Thus the mainstream church can continue to flourish, but it becomes marginal to the rest of society. In such a case, however, it should not be assumed that its position is identical to that of a sect. Although the sect may claim that it has the sole truth and that nobody apart from its own members are saved, only in very exceptional circumstances will the rest of society be so convinced. The sect is therefore very unlikely to be organized on the assumption that it has a responsibility for the moral and spiritual welfare of the whole society in which it is found. In particular, it may proselytize so as to encourage outsiders to attend its services with a view to their becoming converted: but if the outsider fails to respond to the message, then he or she remains one of the damned. By contrast, the mainstream churches have characteristically sought a much greater social outreach and have been organized on that basis. They do not retreat totally to the periphery of society: they may consider themselves and be considered as important opinion leaders in a society where most claim to be Christian, however nominally; and as such they may continue to receive attention in the media. The organizational and architectural structure of the mainstream church will be based upon the assumption of a widespread influence upon society; but in the recent past it has had to come to terms with the implications of shrinking congregations, as well as population shifts. A further difference is that the mainstream church, even on the periphery, will retain doctrinal continuity with its earlier theological outlook. Some of the clergy may develop their theology in a radical direction, but the bulk of the laity will remain fairly conservative (Towler and Coxon, 1979, pp. 200-1). Their beliefs will display some tension with those of the secular social order, but they will not be propounding any new revelation.

It has been clearly documented that the mass of the urban working classes have never had a high degree of active church involvement (Inglis, 1963; Wickham, 1958). There has been considerable discussion of the organization and mission of the urban church,from within church circles, especially Anglican (Paul, 1964; Archbishop of Canterbury's Commission on Urban Priority Areas, 1985). But recently the position of the rural church has also been seen as problematic (Diocese of Lincoln, 1990; Faith in the Countryside, 1990; Francis, 1985) and the myth of the mass of a devout rural population in the past has also been challenged in the countryside. It has further been suggested that for Anglicanism, the ideal of a resident clergyman for every parish was often not realized. Nonetheless, in the rural area, the church building is sometimes highly conspicuous (even if closed); and when church- or chapel-related activities continue, these may be among the more active village-based organizations (Winter, 1991, p. 201).

Although there is much evidence of decline in church involvement, the trend does not seem to be towards the total elimination of the church. Gilbert (1980) speaks in terms of a 'post-Christian society', but maintains that such a society

> is not one from which Christianity has departed, but one in which it has become marginal. It is a society where to be irreligious is to be normal, where to think and act in secular terms is to be conventional, where neither status nor respectability depends upon the practice or profession of religious faith. Some members of such a society continue to find Christianity a profound, vital influence in their lives, but in so doing they place themselves outside the

mainstream of social life and culture ... They become a sub-culture (Gilbert, 1980, p. ix).

In their evaluation of statistical evidence, Currie, Gilbert and Horsley comment likewise:

> there comes a point in the organization's decline at which the external constituency has virtually ceased to exist, and recruitment can arise *only* from within the families of church members. If it be assumed that membership retention continues to fall, even among church members' children, then the recessive phase must conclude in the extinction of the organization. However, the procedures, capital and tradition of an organization may be said to create, among its last few members, an inertia which prevents them from abandoning it altogether while a few random recruits can be brought in from outside (Currie, Gilbert and Horsley, 1977).

Churches, and for that matter secular movements, can continue therefore to attract some following even if they are seen as irrelevant by the wider society (cf. Messinger, 1955; Forster, 1982). But what is particularly interesting in the case of the mainstream church in the West is the move from the centre to the periphery (Wilson, 1966). It is true that even the mainstream church has always been torn between the accommodation of the 'church' and the extremism of the 'sect' (cf. Troeltsch, 1931, esp. pp. 331-3 and pp. 338-41). But if a claim for wider social significance is maintained, tension is likely to develop between the accommodation to the secular world that such a standpoint is likely to require, and the faith of an active, committed remnant. The problem is more acute for some churches than for others. It may for instance turn out to be the case that Anglicanism encounters particular difficulties here. In the recent past, many Anglican churches have tended to reduce the number of services on offer, and may as a consequence concentrate upon the Eucharist. However, full participation in Holy Communion is confined to those who are confirmed.

The national situation

Much of the available statistical evidence for Britain points to a continued decline in church-based 'religiosity' (by whatever criterion is taken) in the twentieth century. There is not totally a unilinear pattern. Argyle (1958, pp. 23-7) points to some evidence for a slight religious revival in the 1950s, by the standard of church membership and similar criteria: and Hastings also notes this temporary respite for the church (Hastings, 1986, pp. 443-7). The Roman Catholics were for a long time an exception to the tendency of church involvement to decline, but since the 1960s they too have followed the same pattern. There is widespread statistical documentation of the tendency for the recent past (Wilson, 1966; Currie, Gilbert, Horsley, 1977). As already noted, the decline has been uneven. Over half the population have until recently married in church, a much higher proportion have been baptized, and funerals without religious rites are still a rarity. Until relatively recently it was common for parents to send their children to Sunday School. But even some of these indicators now show a decline. Currie, Gilbert and Horsley (1977, pp. 87-9) have traced the decline of Sunday Schools since the 1920s. They suggest that sooner or later, withdrawal of adults from church attendance will have implications for children's practice. If parents attend, church membership will also be sought by young people as a sign of adult status. But if most parents are not attenders, then churchgoing will be seen as not the norm, or the norm for children only (Currie, Gilbert and Horsley, 1977, p. 91). The relationship between young people and the church remains important and problematical. Recent survey material also points to the decline in religiosity of the young (See Table 4 below, and Chapter 1 of this volume).

As already noted, there is much evidence of further decline in religious allegiance in the 1970s and 1980s. Using material from the *UK Christian Handbook* (Brierley, 1988), Davie traces the decline in membership of the mainstream churches between 1970 and 1987. The figures are shown in Table 1, which has been adapted to include the figures for 1990 (taken from Brierley and Longley, 1991). The figures are based on membership where such a category exists, upon the Electoral Roll for Anglicans, and upon mass attendance for Roman Catholics. In all cases only those over 15 are included.

These figures show that there has been a steady overall decline in membership for most churches; and this process is now occurring for the Roman Catholics as well. There are however some interesting exceptions. The Baptists appeared to be sharing in the overall decline initially, but the process now seems to have been arrested, and there has been a slight expansion in the recent past. There has also been some expansion for the 'other' churches, and for the Orthodox church. It thus appears that the smaller bodies, of which some but not all have an important ethnic minority constituency, are expanding while the mainstream churches decline. It should be remembered that these are

Table 1
Total UK church members

	1970	1973	1980	1985	1987	1990
Anglican	2,547,767	2,270,028	2,153,854	1,985,367	1,927,506	1,838,659
Methodist	694,333	614,729	558,264	526,432	516,739	483,387
Baptist	295,341	270,259	239,874	239,217	241,451	241,842
Presbyterian	1,806,736	1,645,548	1,508,509	1,383,064	1,346,366	1,291,672
Other Churches	529,728	526,403	532,674	572,904	604,458	697,997
Total Protestant	5,873,905	5,326,967	4,993,175	4,706,984	4,636,520	4,553,557
Roman Catholic	2,714,520	2,534,395	2,342,264	2,127,793	2,059,240	1,945,626
Orthodox	193,430	201,500	208,940	220,036	231,070	265,258
Total Christian	8,781,855	8,062,862	7,544,379	7,054,813	6,926,830	6,764,441
Percentage of adult popultn.	20.7%	18.6%	16.9%	15.3%	15.0%	14.6%

UK figures. Membership of churches is much lower in England than in Scotland, Wales or Northern Ireland: in 1985 only 11 per cent of the English population were church members. None the less, this may be a minority but it shows that church activity is quite a significant minority pursuit.

Table 2 shows the figures for total community. These are also quoted by Davie, but derived from Brierley.[1]

Thus it appears that nominal allegiance to some form of Christianity is quite considerable, though there has also been a decline in even this level of commitment from 72 per cent in 1970 to 65 per cent in 1987. The figure for those with some religious allegiance has however hardly declined at all for the same period (from 75 per cent to 73 per cent; this seems to be due to the growth in the proportion of the population with some allegiance to a non-Christian religion - a rise from 3.0 per cent in 1970 to 7.5 per cent in 1987). By 1985 there were more Muslims in the UK than there were Methodists. It is also interesting that the total number of baptized Roman Catholics has not shrunk as a proportion of the population, for the same period: even though there has been a steady decline in Roman Catholic church involvement. About one-quarter of the population do not count as members of a religious community. This group has increased only slightly as a proportion of

Table 2
Total community figures (millions)

	1970	1975	1980	1983	1985	1987
Church of England	27.8	27.5	26.6	26.1	25.7	25.6
Other Anglican	1.6	1.5	1.4	1.3	1.3	1.3
Baptist	0.6	0.6	0.6	0.6	0.6	0.6
Methodist	1.7	1.6	1.5	1.4	1.3	1.3
Presbyterian	2.1	1.9	1.7	1.7	1.7	1.7
Roman Catholic	5.2	5.2	5.2	5.2	5.2	5.2
Orthodox	0.3	0.4	0.4	0.4	0.4	0.5
Other Trinitarian	1.1	1.1	1.0	1.1	1.2	1.3
Total Trinitarian	40.4	39.8	38.4	37.8	37.4	37.5
Scientology	0.1	0.3	0.5	0.5	0.5	0.6
Other Non-Trinitarian	0.6	0.7	0.7	0.7	0.8	0.8
Jews	0.4	0.4	0.4	0.4	0.3	0.3
Hindus	0.1	0.2	0.3	0.3	0.3	0.3
Muslims	0.3	0.5	1.2	1.3	1.5	1.5
Sikhs	0.1	0.2	0.4	0.4	0.5	0.5
Other Religions	0.1	0.1	0.2	0.2	0.3	0.3
Total Non-Trinitarian and Other Religions	1.7	2.4	3.7	3.8	4.2	4.3
Total All Religions	42.1	42.2	42.1	41.6	41.6	41.8
Percentage Total Christian Churches of Population	72%	71%	68%	67%	66%	65%
Percentage Total All Religions of Population	75%	75%	75%	74%	73%	73%

the population, for the period under consideration. Those of 'no religion' constitute a mixed category, as Chapter 5 in this collection demonstrates in particular.

Brierley and his colleagues give more detailed information in the study *Prospects for the Nineties* (Brierley, 1991). The surveys reported cover attendance as well as membership, and the results are particularly useful because they are given for counties as well as for the total population. For England as a whole in 1989, the figure of 10 per cent is quoted as an indication of adult church attenders as a proportion of the total adult population. The national breakdown by denomination, for adult attenders, is shown in Table 3 (Brierley and Longley, 1991, p. 20).

These figures show that the decline in church attendance in England has continued, but that during the period 1985-9 it has almost levelled off. There are significant differences according to which church is under consideration, but on the whole the pattern is one in which the larger churches have declined but the smaller ones have expanded. It must be remembered that the categories 'Independent', 'Afro-Caribbean' and 'Pentecostal' include a large number of small organizations. These figures confirm that the Baptists are an exception in that they are a relatively large church (e.g. larger than the United Reformed) but have succeeded in achieving some expansion.

A wider range of variables is considered in the European Values Survey. There is separate British data for this, excluding Northern Ireland, and the information is available only for 1981 (Abrams, Gerard, in Abrams, Gerard and Timms, 1985). An interesting feature of these data concerns the decline of religion among the younger age-groups. The figures in Table 4 indicate this.

This is not automatically to be interpreted as evidence of secularization. Another possibility is that religiosity increases as people get older.

Other interesting data from the same survey show that 58 per cent of the British define themselves as 'religious', and 45 per cent believe in a life after death (Gerard in Abrams, Gerard and Timms, Table 3.1, at p. 60). 31 per cent believe in a personal God, while 39 per cent believe in a God, but conceive of the deity in terms of a kind of spirit or life force. 14 per cent see religious faith as an important value to develop in children. The latter attitude is particularly strong among those who think in terms of a personal God. There is also a link between age and acceptance of a personal God. Less than one-fifth of those under 25 see God in personal terms, but half of those aged over 75 hold such a belief (Gerard, 1985, p. 65).

Table 3
Adult church attendance, England, 1989

(a) Free and Episcopal Churches

	Free Churches	Anglican	Roman Catholic	Orthodox	Total Christian
1975	1,209,000	1,302,000	1,576,000	6000	4,093,000
4 yrs change	+3%	-4%	-4%	+17%	-2%
1979	1,247,000	1,256,000	1,515,000	7000	4,025,000
6 yrs change	-1%	-6%	-12%	+20%	-7%
1985	1,229,700	1,181,000	1,335,900	8400	3,755,000
4 yrs change	+2%	-3%	-2%	+12%	-1%
1989	1,249,000	1,143,900	1,304,600	9400	3,706,900
change 1975-89	+3%	-12%	-17%	+57%	-9%

(b) Free Churches: breakdown by denomination

	Methodist	Baptist	United Reformed	Independent	Afro-Caribbean	Pentecostal	Other
1975	454000	193000	150000	167000	55000	78000	112000
4 yrs change	-2%	+5%	-7%	+23%	+20%	+13%	-12%
1979	447000	203000	139000	206000	66000	88000	98000
6 yrs change	-6%	-3%	-13%	+25%	+2%	-4%	-17%
1985	420800	196200	121400	257500	67500	84900	81400
4 yrs change	-6%	+2%	-6%	+14%	+1%	+11%	+2%
1989	396100	199400	114000	292800	68500	95200	83000
change 1975-89	-13%	+3%	-24%	+75%	+25%	+22%	-26%

Table 4
Age and endorsement of traditional religious values,
Great Britain, 1981

		Age		
	Total	18-34	35-54	55+
Believe in God	76%	65%	79%	85%
Derive Comfort and Strength from Religion	46%	28%	46%	67%
Member of Religious Organization	22%	15%	21%	32%
Weekly Church Attendance	14%	10%	13%	20%

(adapted from Table 2.6, Abrams, 1985, p. 32).

The national statistical material here considered therefore confirms the overall impression of mass indifference (not hostility), but with the church continuing to be important as a minority activity. However, the young are less 'religious' than the old, and it remains a matter of speculation for the future whether a plateau has been reached, or whether the masses will be more indifferent, and/or the churches will be pushed further and further to the periphery. The growth of the smaller religious bodies is of interest, but even if their numbers are taken as a whole, they do not compensate for the continued decline in support for the mainstream churches. It is now appropriate to consider how far these trends are replicated locally in Humberside and Lincolnshire.

The local situation: Humberside[2] and Lincolnshire

Hull (population 262,900 in 1991) now promotes itself as the 'Capital of Humberside'. In the past it had been the largest settlement in the East Riding of Yorkshire. However in 1974, the former East Riding joined the new county of Humberside, together with parts of north Lincolnshire. Hull owes its existence and development to the maritime trade, an activity which dates from the fourteenth century. Continued development has been based on the city's position as a trading centre with the European continent. By the eighteenth century Hull had become the main outlet for Yorkshire's industries.

There was a major expansion in the nineteenth century; in 1801 the population of the municipal borough was 22,161, but by 1851 this had risen to 84,690 and by 1881 to 154,240. The process of industrialization overall led to increasing demand for raw materials; Hull had established trading links and was therefore in a good position to import these. Much of the influx of population in the nineteenth century was drawn from the surrounding countryside, but there was some movement from further afield. In the recent past, the city has suffered from decline of trawling, but there have been major redevelopments in the 1980s and 1990s, including some tourist development.

The rural area surrounding Hull depends very largely on agriculture, and the larger urban centres such as Beverley and Driffield are market towns. There is a gas terminal on the coast at Easington.

Lincolnshire presents a very different picture from the City of Hull, but there are some resemblances to the former East Riding. The two banks of the River Humber have been linked by a road bridge since 1981, of which the benefits compared to the costs are still the subject of controversy. On the south side of the Humber, there are ports at Grimsby and Immingham, but the maritime tradition developed only at the beginning of the nineteenth century, much later than in Hull. The impact of the industrial revolution was less than was found on North Humberside; even the City of Lincoln (population 80,900 in 1991) has industries which are mainly linked to an agricultural economy. Tourism also is important to the region.

In order to place the studies in subsequent chapters in context, it is appropriate to examine the religious history of the area under consideration.[3] As far as Hull is concerned, it can be ascertained that recusancy following the Reformation was minimal; most Roman Catholics are immigrants to Hull, or their descendants. The Protestant, and especially Nonconformist, tradition in Hull began in the sixteenth century. Because of Hull's maritime links, dissent was linked to the Continent, as well as to other parts of England. After initial persecution and later toleration, dissenters were free to grow, but this growth was often impaired by internal disagreements.

From the early 1750s, John Wesley was a frequent visitor to Hull, and during this time Methodism became firmly established; by 1771 Hull had become a circuit town. In the later eighteenth century Hull played an important part in the formation of the Methodist New Connexion. There was further growth of Nonconformity in general, and Methodism in particular, in Hull in the nineteenth century. The Methodists were divided between the Wesleyans, whose numbers included many wealthy and influential figures, and the Primitives, who had working-class support. The growth of the working-class population enabled the Primitive Methodists to expand considerably; Hull became their mission centre for the north of England.

Hull also experienced the evangelical revival, and its spirit was reflected in the Anglican churches. In the nineteenth century there was direct competition between Anglican and Methodist churches. Table 5 shows the figures for the 1851 Religious Census.

Table 5
Hull in the 1851 Religious Census
(based on area of modern borough)

Denomination/ religion	No. of churches/ chapels	Sittings	Morning	Attendance Afternoon	Evening
Church of England	18	14020	5933	1182	5114
Roman Catholic	1	648	1050	...	600
Jewish	1	95	74	17	21
Nonconformist	38	23968	9591	1836	12965
Breakdown of Nonconformists by denomination/sect					
Independents	6	4966	1517	80	2083
Baptists	4	1140	425	...	501
Wesleyans	10	8212	3222	71	4113
Primitive Methodists	5	2838	2180	...	2782
Independent Methodists	1	682	450	350	500
Methodist New Connexion	2	1080	410	...	380
Wesleyan Reformed Methodists	1	1000	200	500	1000
Lutherans	1	500	200	...	...
Unitarians	1	490	155	...	130
Presbyterians	1	600	117	...	89
Friends	1	386	111	6	...
Free Church of England	1	330	150	...	300
Latter Day Saints	1	500	70	90	150
Sailors' Chapel	1	500	74	278	130
Disciples of Christ	1	34	10	6	7
Undenominational	1	710	300	400	800

These figures show the strength of Nonconformity, especially Methodism. But Anglicanism also remained strong, and even the Roman Catholics were far from insignificant. During the first half of the nineteenth century the population of Hull had of course increased nearly fourfold.

Church growth in the second half of the nineteenth century continued, and again there was major increase in population. By 1881 the population had reached 154,240, and by 1901 it was 240,259 (since 1881, figures have been for the Municipal Borough). Competition between Anglicans and Methodists continued, with the aim of attracting the new urban population. This process went on until well into the twentieth century, when new chapels and churches were built to keep pace with residential development. The Anglicans were less successful than the Methodists in increasing their numbers. Between 1870 and 1920, the Wesleyans increased their attendance by 54 per cent, and the Primitive Methodists by 75 per cent; but the Anglican increase was only of the order of 12 per cent. The Roman Catholics also grew in the second half of the nineteenth century, with the arrival of 3,000 Irish immigrants. Many churches suffered severe setbacks in the Second World War; the city suffered heavy bombing and several churches were destroyed in this way.

The countryside around Hull, formerly known as the East Riding of Yorkshire, experienced many of the same processes that occurred in the city of Hull. However, Christianity had a much more significant historic role, with Beverley Minster dating from the eighth century. As in the City of Hull, very few retained the Roman Catholic faith after the Reformation. After the eighteenth century, evangelical Christianity held sway. Partly in response to Anglican neglect, the East Riding became more strongly affected by the Methodist Revival than almost anywhere else in England. The legacy of this is still evident: nearly all villages in the region have at least one Methodist chapel; and Methodism also had a wider impact upon social and political life. Wesley preached in nearly all East Riding villages. In the nineteenth century he was followed by Primitive Methodist preachers, notably William Clowes. The Primitive Methodists achieved a substantial following among Wolds farm labourers and coastal fishermen.

Across the river in Lincolnshire,[4] we are again confronted with a rural society with church buildings of historic importance, especially Lincoln Cathedral. However, unlike the East Riding, Roman Catholicism remained in some of the more remote areas after the Reformation, especially when the local landlord supported or even stipulated this. But the competition between Anglicans and Methodists was again very much in evidence, with Nonconformists responding to Anglican neglect (non-resident clergy being a particular problem). By the mid-nineteenth century the Anglicans were responding to the Methodist challenge, but with limited effect. Several parts of Lincolnshire became predominantly Methodist; and Lincolnshire is significant for Methodism in that it contains Epworth, John Wesley's birthplace. Wesleyan congregations probably reflected fairly closely the social composition of the general population, since they included substantial numbers of labourers. The Primitive Methodists were also active, but especially initially they took on more of a sectarian character. However, for some they did provide a religious counter-culture which offered an alternative to the new social order, the older village culture, and the Established Church (Obelkevich, 1976, pp. 257-8).

It now remains to consider the recent statistical evidence for the region under consideration, so as to see how it compares and contrasts with national data. The only reliable guide is provided by Brierley (1991) with figures collected and presented on the same basis as was shown in Table 3. Table 6 shows the Humberside adult attendance figures, and Table 7 the same figures for Lincolnshire. In both cases the figure is lower than the 1989 national average of 10 per cent (7 per cent for Humberside and 9 per cent for Lincolnshire). No Afro-Caribbean or Orthodox churches are reported in either area.

The comparisons and contrasts with the national situation are of great interest. The ethnic minority population of the two regions is fairly low, thus Afro-Caribbean churches do not appear. In many other respects the pattern is very similar to that which is occurring nationally. In most cases the larger bodies, except the Baptists, are declining, but there are two interesting exceptions. In the case of Humberside, there has been a steady increase in Roman Catholic church attendance since 1975. The reason for this is uncertain. Another significant difference is that, for Lincolnshire, since 1985 the decline in Anglican churchgoing has been arrested, and there has been an increase between 1985 and 1989. It is also noteworthy that, while the increase in Baptist church attendance is in accordance with the national pattern, it has occurred on a much greater scale in both Lincolnshire and Humberside. The increase is of the order of 40 per cent for 1975-89 in Lincolnshire, and as high as 140 per cent for Humberside. In both cases, however, the overall picture is of decline in church attendance. In Humberside for 1975-89 this is of the order of only 1 per cent, but for Lincolnshire the figure is as high as 14 per cent.

The studies in this collection are all based on empirical research in the Humberside and Lincolnshire area. All the research in question has been done in the 1980s and 1990s, by staff and postgraduate

xxvii

students of the Department of Sociology and Social Anthropology of the University of Hull. This Department has strong international links, but this in no way implies that the local area has been neglected. Of particular note are Tunstall's work on trawlermen (Tunstall, 1962), Peel on family planning (Peel, 1970, 1972, 1973), Weir on white-collar workers (Weir, 1972, 1973; Mercer and Weir, 1972), and O'Neill on occupational values (O'Neill, 1982). Clarricoates has published several articles on gender stereotyping in primary schools (1978, 1980, 1987, 1988), which are based on a PhD thesis concerned with the local area (Clarricoates, 1984). Also noteworthy is Cunnison (1985), a study of women teachers and trade unionism. This was based on research done at the neighbouring University of Humberside, but was published as an Occasional Paper of the Department of Sociology and Social Anthropology of the University of Hull.

Some of these make incidental reference to religion. Tunstall points out that Hull trawlermen were most unlikely to have any church involvement. However, the extreme and hazardous nature of their occupation made it rare for them to be atheists; they would often pray at times of danger, and the ship's New Testament would not be read but nor would it be defaced. Also, certain kinds of religious blaspheming were disapproved of while on the trawler (1962, pp. 169-70).

O'Neill's research did touch on religion but found that few in the occupational groups examined had any strong views on the subject (1982, pp. 54, 149). Peel, however, points out that religion is important in influencing choices concerning birth control (1970, pp. 52-3, 68-9; 1972, p. 335). Those involved in his survey of married couples in Hull who identified themselves as Roman Catholics were found to take the church's teaching with a degree of seriousness: they tended to want larger families and were more likely to eschew mechanical forms of birth control. The influence of the church was however attenuated somewhat during the marriage; and another factor was that 71 per cent of Catholics were married to a non-Catholic spouse. Another point of interest in Peel's findings is that those active in churches of any kind are likely to want families slightly larger than average.

Shaw and Carr-Hill have recently conducted a local study concerning attitudes to the Gulf War. This covers a wide range of variables, and the extent to which religion influences respondents' attitudes is discussed in Chapter 5 of this collection.

Table 6
Adult church attendance, Humberside, 1989
(adapted from Brierley, 1991, p. 112)

(a) Free and Episcopal Churches

	Free Churches	Anglican	Roman Catholic	Total Christian
1975	19600	16000	12000	47600
4 yrs change	-5%	0%	+3%	-1%
1979	18700	16000	12400	47100
6 yrs change	+3%	-5%	+4%	0%
1985	19200	15200	12900	47300
4 yrs change	+1%	-3%	+2%	0%
1989	19400	14800	13100	47300
change 1975-89	-1%	-8%	+9%	-1%

(b) Free churches: breakdown by denomination

	Methodist	Baptist	United Reformed	Independent	Pentecostal	Other
1975	12700	500	1000	1800	1600	2000
4 yrs change	-6%	+20%	0%	+22%	0%	-35%
1979	12000	600	1000	2200	1600	1300
6 yrs change	-1%	+50%	0%	+14%	+13%	-15%
1985	11900	900	1000	2500	1800	1100
4 yrs change	-4%	+33%	-20%	+12%	+22%	-9%
1989	11400	1200	800	2800	2200	1000
change 1975-89	-10%	+140%	-20%	+56%	+38%	-50%

Table 7
Adult church attendance, Lincolnshire, 1989
(adapted from Brierley, 1991, p. 180)

(a) Free and Episcopal Churches

	Free Churches	Anglican	Roman Catholic	Total Christian
1975	15500	26000	6400	47900
4 yrs change	-5%	-12%	-2%	-8%
1979	14800	23000	6300	44100
6 yrs change	-2%	-16%	-2%	-9%
1985	14500	19400	6200	40100
4 yrs change	-7%	+12%	-2%	+3%
1989	13500	21700	6100	41300
change 1975-89	-13%	-17%	-5%	-14%

(b) Free churches: breakdown by denomination

	Methodist	Baptist	United Reformed	Independent	Pentecostal	Other
1975	11000	1000	1000	600	700	1200
4 yrs change	-9%	+20%	-10%	+50%	0%	-8%
1979	10000	1200	900	900	700	1100
6 yrs change	-8%	+8%	-11%	+44%	+14%	0%
1985	9200	1300	800	1300	800	1100
4 yrs change	-13%	+8%	0%	+15%	+13%	-18%
1989	8000	1400	800	1500	900	900
change 1975-89	-27%	+40%	-20%	+150%	+29%	-25%

The present volume incorporates nearly all the research done in the Hull Sociology and Social Anthropology Department concerning the sociology of religion in Britain. The only exceptions are a short survey of ordinands at Lincoln Theological College, conducted by myself (Forster, 1984), and Morgan's thesis on Anglican bishops (Morgan, 1963), which was based on a national study. The research does not form part of an overall 'plan'; all of it is based upon individual projects (though obviously there has been some mutual influence). However, it is hoped that these studies will stimulate further research on mainstream Christianity, both locally and nationally.

Not all the contributors to this collection would go along wholeheartedly with a secularization thesis, but there is nothing in any of the papers to suggest otherwise than religious decline. The decline is not to nothing, and as a peripheral activity church involvement is by no means negligible. When the wider population who are not church attenders are examined, a clear picture emerges of a situation where the young are less religious than the old, no matter what criterion is taken. Also, although the move of the church to the periphery is more evident in the urban than in the rural situation, there is a movement in that direction in rural areas as well. It is useful to examine the contributions in relation to firstly, the mass of the population and secondly, those involved in the church.

The mass of the population

My own study of a council estate shows that even the unchurched mostly do not wish to put themselves beyond the pale. Most will give a religious label when asked, and as many as 47.3 per cent described themselves as 'religious'. This is less than, but quite close to, the 58 per cent affirmative answer to this question in the European Values Survey. Shaw and Carr-Hill are also concerned with the population as a whole, most of whom will turn out to be unchurched. It is of interest that as many as 13 per cent said that they had no religion for the purpose of answering a postal questionnaire, whereas only 3 per cent on Longhill Estate would give this answer if asked about religion on entry to hospital. In their study of the Gulf War, Shaw and Carr-Hill show that denominational labels are not a key factor but are none the less a significant influence upon people's attitudes.

There are other ways in which the church has an impact on the masses of the unchurched. The continued demand for rites of passage has been widely noted. However, my own research suggests that marriage in church is declining among the young though still remains quite popular. Spencer draws attention to an interesting controversy concerning baptism of children of those with no other church interests. It appears that baptism of children is still felt to be 'normal', though some of the clergy are now beginning to challenge popular attitudes. This can cause resentment, even if a thanksgiving is offered as an alternative.[5] It appears that it is less appropriate to think in general terms about rites of passage; each ritual may need separate sociological attention.

Other people who are outside the church may seem to 'support' it in some way. This is noted in Dalling and Francis's study, where certain recreational activities are used to raise funds for the church. The church may also provide a recreational focus as part of its community outreach. One of the clergy studied by Spencer had done this successfully, and Worsfold draws attention to this function of the church in his study of a youth club, in which conflict occurred between those who were and those who were not also interested in religious activities.

Spencer also draws attention to the role of the clergy in relation to the wider community, and this matter is also commented upon in my own study, and by Dalling and Francis. The question of pastoral visitation arises in this connection. Spencer discusses in relation to the Baptist minister the fact that he is concerned with outreach to bring people into his church, rather than feeling responsibility to the community as a whole. This is an interesting comment, to be considered side by side with the growth of the Baptist church nationally and in the area considered here.

Those involved in the church

My own study shows that in a very highly secularized situation, those who remain active in an Anglican church display a high level of involvement. The church, though established, becomes more like a sect: and in this particular case such a development was not discouraged by the priest. It is similarly noted by Worsfold that a fundamentalist, evangelical approach was dominant in the religious activities of an Anglican church youth club. Those with other kinds of actual or potential church commitment can sometimes be discouraged because of this; but in all events, a strong commitment is needed for continued church activity in a highly secularized environment. Dalling and Francis by contrast show that only a weak or even non-existent theistic or Christian belief is needed in order to participate in a rural church. This suggests that the church can retain a high degree of social importance in the rural area, even though the village has also become highly secularized. They also show the social impact of Anglican-Methodist divisions, and they examine the social implications of church closures.

Spencer pays particularly close attention to the relationship between clergy and laity. This involves consideration of matters such as authority vis-a-vis the laity, powers of innovation, and pressures of ministry; denominational differences are also highlighted.

Shaw and Carr-Hill also note that the clergy have distinctive attitudes concerning the Gulf War, but that this varied between denominations; those of the episcopal churches were less pro-war than the general population, though this difference was not apparent with the Nonconformists.

On the whole, then, the material connected locally confirms the national pattern. If the masses are indifferent, and are possibly becoming more so, the relationship between the church and the rest of the population becomes highly problematical in a culture which none the less is historically Christian. This remaining veneer of Christianity is not to be lightly dismissed; people do not like their commitment to be challenged, and those who differ in their denominational allegiance still differ to some extent in their attitudes. Tensions have arisen particularly over the question of whether the clergy are there to serve the population at large or only those with some church connection. Especially for Anglicans, infant baptism has turned out to be a 'political football' over this question, and the issue has received attention locally.[6]   Especially in the mainstream churches, the demands made by the wider population can remain, while the number of clergy and churches declines: with the consequence of heavy demands placed upon the remaining clergy.

The gap between the churches and the masses may well continue to grow. The young seem less 'religious' than the old, no matter what criterion is taken. At the same time there is a tendency for some mainstream churches, now at the periphery of society, either to put forward a version of Christianity which displays considerable tension with the wider society, or to make heavy demands on their members (or in some cases to do both). This represents a move from church to sect, in the opposite direction to the historic pattern.[7] Such a process, it appears, is more likely to occur in the urban situation; even with falling attendance the church can retain social roots in the countryside and maintain a higher social profile.   The effect is that beliefs and activities of those who continue their church involvement are much less in tension with those of the wider society.

Notes

1. The bases upon which 'total community' figures were calculated is discussed in more detail in Brierley and Hiscock, 1993.
2. The status of the County of Humberside has remained controversial from the beginning, and change is anticipated. However, 'Humberside' was the county name in use at the time of the studies made here, and has therefore been retained.
3. Historical information is derived mainly from Allison (1969, esp. pp. 287-332); Harrison, 1973; Pearson, 1947; and Spencer, 1989.
4. Historical information on Lincolnshire is derived from Obelkevich, 1976, and Rogers, 1970.
5. For the local controversy on this subject see *Hull Daily Mail*, 15, 16, 19, 23, 26 and 27 August 1983.
6. Ibid.
7. For the classic statement on this question see Niebuhr, 1929.

References

Abrams, M. (1985), 'Demographic Correlates of Values', in Abrams, Gerard and Timms, pp. 21-49.

Abrams, M., Gerard, D. and Timms, N. (eds.) (1985), *Values and Social Changes in Britain*, Macmillan, Basingstoke.

Allison, K.J. (ed.) (1969), *A History of the County of York East Riding: Vol. 1: The City of Kingston-upon-Hull*, Oxford University Press, London.

Archbishop of Canterbury, Commission on Urban Priority Areas (1985), *Faith in the City: A Call for Action by Church and Nation*, Church House, London.

Argyle, M. (1958), *Religious Behaviour*, Routledge and Kegan Paul, London.

Brierley, P. (ed.) (1988), *UK Christian Handbook, 1989/90*, MARC Europe, Bromley.

Brierley, P. (ed.) (1991), *Prospects for the Nineties: Trends and Tables from the English Church Census - All England, Denominations and Churchmanship*, MARC Europe, London.

Brierley, P. and Longley, D. (1991), *UK Christian Handbook, 1992/3*, MARC Europe, London.

Brierley, P. and Hiscock, V. (1993), *UK Christian Handbook, 1994/5*, Christian Research Association, London.

Clarricoates, K.M. (1978), 'Dinosaurs in the Classroom: A Re-examination of Some Aspects of the "Hidden Curriculum" in Primary Schools', *Women's Studies International Quarterly* 1, pp. 353-364.

Clarricoates, K.M. (1980), 'The Importance of Being Ernest ... Emma ... Tom ... and Jane: The Categorization of Gender in Primary Schools', in R. Deen (ed.), *Schooling for Women's Work*, Routledge and Kegan Paul, London, pp. 26-41. Also (1983) in J. Purvis and M. Hales (eds.), *Achievement and Inequality in Education*, Routledge, London, pp. 193-208.

Clarricoates, K.M. (1984), 'Gender Relations and Teacher-Pupil Interaction in Four Northern Secondary Schools', Hull University PhD.

Clarricoates, K.M. (1987), 'Child Culture at School: A Clash Between Gendered Worlds?, in A. Pollard (ed.), *Children and Their Primary Schools: A New Perspective*, Falmer Press, Lewes, pp. 188-206.

Clarricoates, K.M. (2nd ed., 1988), 'All in a Day's Work', in D. Spender and E. Sarah, *Learning to Lose: Sexism and Education*, Women's Press, London, pp. 69-80.

Cunnison, S. (1985), *Making it in a Man's World: Women Teachers in a Senior High School*, University of Hull, Department of Sociology and Social Anthropology, (Occasional Paper No. 1), Hull.

Currie, R., Gilbert, A. and Horsley, L. (1977), *Churches and Churchgoers: Patterns of Church Growth in the British Isles since 1700*, Clarendon Press, Oxford.

Davie, G. (1990), 'An Ordinary God: The Paradox of Religion in Contemporary Britain', *British Journal of Sociology*, 41, pp. 395-421.

Diocese of Lincoln (1990), *The Challenge of Change in the Countryside, Submission to the Archbishops' Commission on Rural Areas*, Gemini Printers, Boston.

Faith in the Countryside: a Report presented to the Archbishop of Canterbury and York (1990), Churchman Publishing, Worthing.

Forster, P.G. (1972), 'Secularization in the English Context: Some Conceptual and Empirical Problems', *Sociological Review*, 20, pp. 153-68.

Forster, P.G. (1982), *The Esperanto Movement*, Mouton, The Hague.

Forster, P.G. (1984), 'Marriage, Sexuality and the Church: Some Sociological Findings', *Crucible*, Jan. - Mar., pp. 31-40.

Francis, L.J. (1985), *Rural Anglicanism: A Future for Young Christians?*, Collins, London.

Gerard, D. (1985), 'Religious Attitudes and Values', in Abrams, Gerard and Timms, pp. 50-92.

Gilbert, A.D. (1980), *The Making of Post-Christian Britain: A History of the Secularization of Modern Society*, Longman, London.

Harrison, K.K. (1973), 'The Decline of Methodism in Kingston-upon-Hull in this Century', Hull University MA.

Hastings, A. (1986), *A History of English Christianity 1920-1985*, Collins, London.

Horobin, G.W. (1957), 'Community and Occupation in the Hull Fishing Industry', *British Journal of Sociology*, 8, pp. 343-50.

Hull Daily Mail, 15, 16, 19, 23, 26 and 27 August 1983.

Inglis, K.S. (1963), *Churches and the Working Classes in Victorian England*, Routledge and Kegan Paul, London.

MacIntyre, A. (1967), *Secularization and Moral Change*, Oxford University Press, London.

Martin, D.A. (1965), 'Towards Eliminating the Concept of Secularization', in J. Gould (ed.), *Penguin Survey of the Social Sciences*, Penguin, Harmondsworth, pp. 169-82

Martin, D.A. (1967), *A Sociology of English Religion*, SCM, London.

Mercer, D.E. and Weir, D.T.H. (1972), 'Attitudes to Work and Trade Unions among White Collar Workers', *Industrial Relations Journal*, 3 (1), pp. 49-60.

Messinger, S. (1955), 'Organizational Transformation: A Case Study of a Declining Social Movement', *American Sociological Review*, 20, pp. 3-13.

Morgan, D.H.J. (1963), 'Social and Educational Backgrounds of English Diocesan Bishops in the Church of England, 1860-1960' (2 Vols), Hull University MA.

Niebuhr, H.R. (1929), *The Social Sources of Denominationalism*, Holt, New York.

Obelkevich, J. (1976), *Religion in Rural Society: South Lindsey 1825-1875*, Clarendon Press, Oxford.

O'Neill, N. (1982), *Fascism and the Working Class*, Shakti, Southall.

Paul, L.A. (1964), *The Deployment and Payment of the Clergy*, Church Information Office, London.

Pearson, F.R. (1947), *A Brief History of Christianity in East Yorkshire*, East Riding Education Committee, Beverley.

Peel, J. (1970), 'The Hull Family Survey I: The Survey Couples, 1966', *Journal of Biosocial Science*, 2, pp. 45-70.

Peel, J. (1972), 'The Hull Family Survey II: Family Planning in the first five Years of Marriage', *Journal of Biosocial Science*, 4, pp. 330-346.

Peel, J. (1973), 'Patterns of Fertility', *Journal of Biosocial Science*, 5, pp. 241-9.

Rogers, A. (1970), *A History of Lincolnshire with Maps and Pictures*, Darwen Finlayson, Henley-on-Thames.

Social Surveys (Gallup Poll) (1964a), *Television and Religion*, University of London Press, London.

Social Surveys (Gallup Poll) (1964b), *Television and Religion: Full Statistical Tables of a Survey Research from ABC TV*, ABC Television, London.

Spencer, C. (1989), 'The Role of the Clergy in Secular Society', Hull University MPhil.

Towler, R. and Coxon, A.P.M. (1979), *The Fate of the Anglican Clergy: A Sociological Study.* Macmillan: London.

Troeltsch, E. (1931), *The Social Teachings of the Christian Churches*, Eng. trans., Macmillan, New York.

Tunstall, J. (1962), *The Fishermen*, Macgibbon and Kee, London.

Turner, B.S. (1983), *Religion and Social Theory*, Heinemann, London.

Wallis, R. and Bruce, S. (1989), 'Religion: the British Contribution', *British Journal of Sociology*, 40, pp. 493-520.

Weir, D.T.H. (1972), 'Satisfactions in White-Collar Work', in E. Butterworth and D.T.H. Weir, *Social Problems of Modern Britain*, pp. 374-383.

Weir, D.T.H. (1973), 'The Wall of Darkness: Subjective Operationality and the Promotion System among Clerical Workers', in Weir, D.T.H. (ed.), *Men and Work in Modern Britain*, Fontana Collins, London, pp. 169-80.

Wickham, E.R. (1958), *Church and People in an Industrial City*, Lutterworth, Sheffield.

Wilson, B.R. (1966), *Religion in Secular Society*, Watts, London.

Winter, M. (1991), 'The Sociology of Religion and Rural Sociology: A House Divided', *Sociologia Ruralis*, 31, pp. 201-8.

1 Residual religiosity on a Hull council estate

Peter G. Forster

The issue of secularization has been widely discussed among sociologists of religion, and that such a process exists and is likely to continue has been widely assumed. The concept of secularization has admittedly had its critics; thus Martin (1965) has been suspicious of its ideological underpinnings, and Shiner (1967) has suggested that it subsumes some different and analytically separable processes. But nobody has really denied the fact that there has been a decline in religion in Britain throughout the twentieth century, whatever criterion of 'secularization' is taken. More debate has occured, however, on the matter of predictions for the future. Thus whereas Wilson (1966, esp. Part I) has tended to suggest that religion is definitely on the way out, except as a minority activity, Martin (1967, esp. ch. 2) has preferred to maintain that important elements of 'religiosity' still remain, and that the process is not necessarily irreversible. This debate was conducted in the mid-1960s, and sufficient time has now elapsed to enable the investigator to ascertain whether the hypothesis of further secularization can be verified by empirical data. The data presented here deal with the elements of religion that remain in a situation where the church has become marginalized. They concern a Hull council estate. Since council estates are well known to be areas of religious indifference, it is to be expected that they can provide particularly

1

good evidence of secularization, if such a process exists. In investigating such a situation, it is also of especial interest to relate 'religiosity' to age. If it can be shown that 'religiosity' increases with age, then such findings can potentially support a hypothesis of secularization (though as will be indicated, there might be an alternative explanation).

Longhill Estate is on the eastern side of the city and was constructed in the mid to late 1950s. Houses there range in size from two to four bedrooms, in pairs or short terraces; and there are also some low-rise flats. There are two foster-homes and an old people's home. Public spaces include two shopping areas, a library, a playing field and three pubs. There are five schools, but these do not cater for pupils over thirteen. Longhill appears to be a 'medium demand' estate, and the Hull Housing Department receives few requests for transfers to other estates.

The Anglican church on the Estate, St Margaret's, was opened in 1959 to serve as a worship centre and a community hall. It constitutes a daughter church to the parish church of St Michael's, on the nearby main road. For 20 years St Margaret's was served by a series of curates and Church Army personnel, but in 1979 the question of the sale of the church and disposal of the buildings was discussed. The then incumbent resisted that proposal, but in 1980 worship ceased, though a Sunday school continued till 1983. In 1984 worship recommenced on the initiative of a small group of laity, encouraged by clergy from neighbouring parishes. Eucharistic worship recommenced in September 1984, on the appointment of a new incumbent at St Michael's. In November 1986 St Margaret's was rededicated, and a mission priest was appointed to Longhill.

Anglicanism has not been the only Christian presence on Longhill. There was until recently a Roman Catholic church where mass was said, though part of the building had been converted for use by the YTS. Also, the Salvation Army has its own premises, which when this study began were used mainly as a Sunday School.

The survey, whose main results are summarized here, was conducted in 1986, by direct request from church sources, with the aim of providing background information for an Urban Mission Experiment[1]. A sample of 397 individuals eligible to vote was drawn from the Register of Electors. This constituted 7.9 per cent of the total of slightly over 5,000 adults. A total of 207 questionnaires was completed successfully, the response rate therefore being 52.6 per cent of the sample drawn. This is not a particularly good rate for a survey done by personal interviews. However, surveys of religion in the general

2

Table 1.1
Response to survey by age and sex

Age	Male		Female		All
	N	%	N	%	N
17-30	21	53.8	18	46.2	39
31-60	40	41.2	57	58.8	97
61 up	33	48.5	35	51.4	68
No answer	2	(66.7)	1	(33.3)	3
Total	96	46.4	111	53.6	207

population are notoriously difficult to administer, and this result can be seen as reasonably satisfactory. There is some evidence of bias in the sample. There was a better response rate from women (60 per cent) than from men (45.3 per cent). Also, less conclusively, it appears that those who refused to complete the questionnaire were more likely to be hostile to the church and religion than were those who cooperated. This appears to be so since a number of refusals were accompanied by anti-religious remarks. Thus to some unknown degree the results may be biased towards the more 'religious' Estate dwellers. It might therefore turn out that a more representative survey could reveal them as, if anything, less religious than the present findings show.

Before embarking upon religious topics, the survey dealt with some more general issues. It was found that the Estate had built up a fairly stable population. 70.0 per cent of the population had been there over ten years, and only 0.5 per cent for less than one year. Moreover, 52.2 per cent of residents claimed to have a relative living in a house or flat elsewhere on Longhill - quite a high figure for a fairly young community. There was a good deal of satisfaction with the Estate; 81.2 per cent said that they liked living there. Though 35.7 per cent said that the Estate was not safe at night, many who said this stressed that this was a general problem and not something to be blamed upon Longhill.

The recent growth of the Estate is seen in the fact that only 14.0 per cent were brought up on the Estate, and hardly any adults had been born there. However, 78.7 per cent had been born somewhere else in Hull. Examining the age profile, the mean age turns out to be 50.4 (s =

17.3) but this disguises the fact that the 31-50 age group are under-represented. Table 1.1 shows distribution by age and sex.

It was also found that 70.5 per cent were married, and only 11.1 per cent were single. Only 1.9 per cent admitted to cohabiting without marriage. The orthodox nuclear-family pattern is the norm on the Estate; only 3.9 per cent of households had other patterns, such as three-generation households. Only 3.4 per cent of households were one-parent families. The norm of the nuclear family is in a sense symbolized on Longhill by the institutional provision for orphans and old people. Family size does not seem to differ from the general British pattern. It was quite common to have 0 to 3 children, but larger numbers than that were much more unusual.

Table 1.2 shows that the majority of Estate dwellers of all ages had no job.

Table 1.2
Employment by sex

| Age | Male | | Female | | All |
	N	%	N	%	N
No job	56	58.3	71	64.0	127
Job*	0	..	1	0.9	1
Full-time	36	37.5	13	11.7	49
Part-time	3	3.1	25	22.5	28
No answer	1	1.0	1	0.9	2
Total	96		111		207

* One did not indicate whether full- or part-time.

There is no indication as to what proportion were available for work. It is significant, however, that only 50.8 per cent of males under 61 had a job full-time, with a further 4.9 per cent employed part-time.[2] Full-time education for most Longhill residents seems in most cases to have ended at the legal minimum age. Only 7.2 per cent had continued beyond the age of 16. Evidence apart from the survey also shows that Longhill is an area of Hull where a high proportion (27 per cent) receive certificated housing benefit; this suggests that for those in employment, low wages are a common problem. It thus appears that if the criteria of low wages and unemployment are taken, Longhill can be seen as a deprived area; but this is not so by other standards, such as shared dwellings, one-parent families, and lack of exclusive use of a bath and inside toilet.

With this background information in mind it is appropriate to consider religious attitudes, beliefs and participation for Longhill people. It will be seen that the relationship of these to the age of respondents turns out to be of particular interest.

Respondents were asked, 'Would you say you were a religious person, or not religious?', and the answers are shown in Table 1.3, in relation to age.

Table 1.3
Age and declared 'religiosity'

| Age | Considered self 'religious' | | Uncertain | | Considered self 'not religious' | | No answer | | All |
	N	%	N	%	N	%	N	%	N
17-30	7	17.9	1	2.6	31	79.5	0	..	39
31-60	48	49.5	9	9.3	40	41.2	0	..	97
61 up	42	61.8	6	8.8	19	27.9	1	1.5	68
No answer	1	(33.3)	1	(33.3)	1	(33.3)	0	..	3
	98	47.3	17	8.2	91	44.0	1	0.5	207

Significance (omitting the 'uncertain' and both kinds of 'no answers'. $P < 0.005$, $x^2 = 26.43$).

This result can be corroborated by inspection of the mean age for the 'religious' and the 'not religious'. This turns out to be 55.7 for the 'religious' (s = 15.3) and 44.5 for the 'not religious' (s = 18.3) and this difference is highly significant (z = 4.5).

Thus the older Estate dwellers are much more likely than the younger to consider themselves 'religious'. A related question is that concerning belief in God. The question for this was phrased 'Some people wonder whether there is a God or not; how do you feel; do you think there is a God, or not?'. It was designed so as to stress that a non-theistic option was available; the results, again cross-tabulated with age, are presented in Table 1.4.

5

Again, the difference in mean age for theists (55.3, s = 16.5) and for non-theists and the uncertain combined (45.1, s = 17.6) is significant (z = 3.9) and corroborates the fact that belief in God increases with age. It

Table 1.4
Age and theism

	Theist		Uncertain		Non-theist		No answer		All
Age	N	%	N	%	N	%	N	%	N
17-30	17	43.6	8	20.5	14	35.9	0	..	39
31-60	68	70.1	13	13.4	14	14.4	2	2.1	97
61 up	52	76.5	9	13.2	7	10.3	0	"	68
No answer	1	(33.3)	1	(33.3)	1	(33.3)	0	..	3
	138	66.7	31	15.0	36	17.4	2	1.0	207

Significance (omitting both kinds of 'no answers'). P < 0.005. x^2 = 15.43.

is interesting that the big difference is between the 17-30s and the rest. Those who did not believe in God, or who expressed some doubt on the subject, were asked whether they would consider themselves atheists or agnostics. The results are presented in Table 1.5 in relation to age. The question was worded 'Would you say you were an atheist or agnostic then?'.

Omitting the 'no answers', combining atheists and agnostics, and comparing their relationships with age to that of believers, a significant results is obtained (P < 0.005, x^2 = 27.2). The mean age of atheists and agnostics taken together is 44.9 (s = 18.4), while for all others it is 51.9 (s = 16.8). The mean age of atheists and agnostics is seen to be significantly lower than that of other categories (z = 2.2, significant at 0.05 level).

It thus appears that slightly less than one-third of Longhill people were at least doubtful about the existence of God, and slightly less than one-fifth considered themselves atheists or agnostics. In all cases, it was particularly those under 31 who were likely to show some scepticism of theistic claims. However, this does not necessarily apply at the declaratory level. When asked for a religious label nearly all Longhill people were prepared to give one, regardless of age.

Table 1.5
Age, atheism and agnosticism

Age	Atheist		Agnostic		Total atheist plus agnostic		All others		Grand total
	N	%	N	%	N	%	N	%	N
17-30	7	17.9	9	23.1	16	41.0	23	59.0	39
31-60	5	5.2	6	6.2	11	11.3	86	88.7	97
61 up	3	4.4	6	8.8	9	13.2	59	86.8	68
No answer	0	..	2	(66.7)	2	(66.7)	1	(33.3)	3
	15	7.2	23	11.1	38	18.4	169	81.6	207

Table 1.6
Declared religious allegiance on entry to hospital

	N	All respondents %
Church of England	160	77.3
Methodist	10	4.8
Roman Catholic	19	9.2
Presbyterian	3	1.4
Baptist	2	1.0
Salvation Army	1	0.4
Mormon	1	0.4
Christian	2	1.0
Atheist/agnostic	3	1.4
None/leave blank	4	1.9
No answer to the question	2	1.0
	207	

Table 1.6 shows the answers to the question 'If a hospital or similar institution asked you to write your religion on a form, what would you put down?'. There was no meaningful relationship with age for answers to this question.

It was noted that 79.1 per cent of those who did not believe in or were uncertain of the existence of God would put themselves down as 'Church of England', and this was true of 84.2 per cent of the atheists and agnostics. These results show that public display of scepticism is avoided, even by those who see themselves as atheists and agnostics. One respondent was quite explicit about the matter. He was generally secularistic in his replies to questions on religion, but said 'bloody Christian, I suppose!' in answer to this question.

In view of this support for Christianity at a declaratory level,[3] it is useful also to consider respondents' attitudes to Christianity and to some of its central components. The first question of this kind was 'How do you regard Christianity? Can you tell me which of these comes nearest to your opinion?'. A card was shown with answers in terms of 'the truest religion', 'as true as any others', 'unimportant' and 'rubbish'. Table 1.7 shows that there was an important relationship

Table 1.7
Age and attitude to Christianity

Age	Truest religion		As true as others		Unimportant or rubbish		Don't know		No answer		All
	N	%	N	%	N	%	N	%	N	%	N
17-30	4	10.2	18	46.2	13	33.4	2	5.1	2	5.1	39
31-60	27	27.8	55	56.7	11	11.4	1	1.0	3	3.1	97
61 up	33	48.5	28	41.2	5	7.4	1	1.5	1	1.5	68
No answer	1	(33.3)	1	(33.3)	1	(33.3)	0	..	0	..	3
	65	31.4	102	49.3	30	14.5	4	6	6	2.9	207

9

between answers to this question and age. Omitting the 'don't knows' and both kinds of 'no answers' these results are statistically significant ($P < 0.005$, $x^2 = 27.8$). Moreover, the mean age for those saying that Christianity was the truest religion was 57.7 ($s = 16.4$) as opposed to a mean age of 47.1 ($s = 16.6$) for all other answers. This difference is also significant ($z = 4.3$). It can therefore be demonstrated that the younger age-groups were more likely to be sceptical of Christianity, though even among the 17-30s only about one-third saw it as unimportant or rubbish. Older people were, however, more likely to see Christianity as having unique claims, while younger people more often saw it as one religion among many.

A component of attitudes to Christianity which bears a significant relationship to age is the question of the Bible. About three-quarters (76.3 per cent) of the households in which a respondent lived had a Bible. However, 62.0 per cent of respondents said that they never read it. The Bible was typically acquired as a present or prize, during the respondent's youth. It appears that though Bibles were seldom read, they were not discarded. When Longhill people were asked about their *attitude* to the Bible, a significant relationship with age was found. Respondents were asked 'How do you see the Bible?', and a card invited them to choose between alternatives in terms of being 'dictated' by God, 'inspired' by God, 'about God', 'literature' or 'fairy stories'. The results are shown in Table 1.8.

The relationship here is not significant if the 31-60s and the over-61s are considered separately. However, if these two age-groups are combined and then compared with the 17-30s, a significant relationship can be detected. If 'don't knows' and both kinds of 'no answers' are omitted, then $P < 0.05$ and $x^2 = 4.0$. Thus it is shown that the over-31s were significantly more likely to subscribe to the idea of some form of divine intervention in the writing of the Bible than were the 17-30s. Moreover, the mean age of those who saw the Bible as inspired or dictated by God was found to be 54.1 ($s = 16.8$), while for those who saw it as being about God, literature or fairy stories, it was 46.6 ($s = 17.3$). This difference is also significant ($z = 3.1$).

Respondents were also asked 'Do you get comfort and strength from religion, or not?'. The results are presented in Table 1.9.

If 'don't knows' and both kinds of 'no answers' are omitted a significant result is obtained ($P < 0.005$, $x^2 = 5.8$). Thus it is shown that there was a general growth with age of the feeling that religion provided a source of comfort and strength. Moreover the mean age of those who derived such comfort and strength was 55.9 ($s = 15.2$), but was 45.2 ($s = 18.1$) for those who did not do so. This difference is also significant ($z = 4.4$).

Table 1.8
Age and attitude to the Bible

Age	Inspired or dictated by God N	%	About God/literature/fairy stories N	%	Don't know N	%	No answer N	%	All N
17-30	13	33.3	24	61.5	1	2.6	1	2.6	39
31-60	46	47.4	46	47.4	2	2.1	3	3.1	97
61 up	39	57.3	28	41.2	0	...	1	1.6	68
No answer	1	(33.3)	2	(66.7)	0	...	0	...	3
	99	47.8	100	48.3	3	1.4	5	2.4	207

Table 1.9
Age and derivation of comfort and strength from religion

Age	Yes, comfort and strength N	%	No comfort and strength N	%	Don't know N	%	No answer N	%	All N
17-30	8	20.5	28	71.8	1	2.6	2	5.1	39
31-60	44	45.4	46	47.4	4	4.1	3	3.1	97
61 up	39	57.4	22	32.4	5	7.4	2	2.9	68
No answer	1	(33.3)	1	(33.3)	0	...	1	(33.3)	3
	92	44.4	97	46.9	10	4.8	8	2.9	207

Table 1.10
Age and private prayer

Age	Pray N	Pray %	Do not pray N	Do not pray %	No answer N	No answer %	All N
17-30	9	23.1	27	69.2	3	7.7	39
31-60	58	59.8	35	36.1	4	4.1	97
61up	41	60.3	24	35.3	3	4.4	68
No answer	1	(33.3)	1	(33.3)	1	(33.3)	3
	109	52.7	87	42.0	11	5.3	207

So far the concern has been mainly with beliefs and attitudes. It is worthwhile also to look at the question of religious practice; this involves both attendance at normal services and use of the church for rites of passage. In Longhill the former is of very little importance, the latter much more so. First, however, it is of interest to examine private prayer. The relationship with age is shown in Table 1.10. The question was 'Do you ever pray privately, at home or elsewhere?'.

Omitting both kinds of 'no answers', the difference shown here can be seen to be statistically significant ($P < 0.005$, $x^2 = 16.9$). Moreover, the difference in the mean age of those who claimed to pray (53.8, s = 15.7) and those who did not (46.7, s = 18.7) is also significant. Once again, the key difference is between the 17-30s and the over-31s. About three-fifths of the over-31s claimed private prayer, but this was true of less than one-quarter of the 17-30s.

On the matter of church attendance, respondents were asked "Do you ever go to church apart from times such as weddings and funerals?'. If yes, they were asked 'How often?'. Few reported much activity; only 6.8 per cent said that they attended monthly or more frequently, while a further 22.2 per cent claimed at least some, less frequent attendance. 4.8 per cent did not answer, while the remaining 66.2 per cent said they never attended. An examination was made of the relationship between age and the difference between those who never attended and those who attended at least sometimes. The relationship is presented in Table 1.11.

This is an interesting departure from the normal pattern of increased 'religiosity' with age. Those who were more likely to declare at least some church attendance tended to come from the middle age-group rather than from the elderly. These results are, however, not quite significant at the level of $P < 0.05$ (omitting both kinds of 'no answers', $x^2 = 5.9$). There is also no significant difference between the mean age of those who never attend and those who attend at least sometimes. Thus it seems that the relationship between age and church attendance is not very strong. However, some claimed that they used to attend, or that they used to attend more often. The question was worded 'Did you ever go to church?' (with the words 'more often' added for those who still reported some attendance). The results for this question are presented in Table 1.12, showing the relationship with age.

Table 1.11
Age and church attendance

Age	Never attend		Attend at least sometimes		No answer		All
---	N	%	N	%	N	%	N
17-30	31	79.4	7	17.9	1	2.6	39
31-60	54	55.7	34	35.1	9	9.3	97
61up	50	73.5	18	26.5	0	...	68
No answer	2	(66.7)	1	(33.3)	0	...	3
	137	66.2	60	29.0	10	4.8	207

Table 1.12
Age and previous church attendance

Age	Yes, did attend		No, did not attend		No answer		All
---	N	%	N	%	N	%	N
17-30	20	51.2	18	46.2	1	2.6	39
31-60	77	79.4	16	16.5	4	4.1	97
61up	54	79.4	7	10.3	7	10.3	68
No answer	2	(66.7)	1	(33.3)	0	...	3
	153	73.9	42	20.3	12	5.8	207

There is no significant difference in mean age of those who had previously attended church and those who had not. Moreover, Table 1.11 shows that as large a proportion of the 31-60s had attended church (more) in the past as of the over-61s. However, if all those over 31 are compared with the 17-30s, then a significant difference emerges (omitting both kinds of 'no answers', $P < 0.005$, $x^2 = 19.1$). Thus although over half in all age-groups reported that they had attended church more in the past, this claim was less commonly made by the 17-30s. None the less, even most of the younger people had had some contact with the church, probably of a compulsory kind, which had been dropped when older. Respondents were asked to give their reasons for ceasing attendance. The commonest answers were that church involvement was a phenomenon of younger years of life, something to be dropped as part of the process of growing up. Often there was indication of some kind of compulsion, from parents, school, the armed forces, or the Scouts and Guides. When these were left behind, churchgoing was too. Other reasons given for ceasing attendance were change of residence, the closure of a particular church, or pressure from work.

But while normal church attendance was very sparse, a different picture emerged with rites of passage. It is well known that non-churchgoers still use the church for such purposes; but it is important to look at each transition separately. Thus *christening* was seen as virtually automatic. Only one respondent claimed not to have been christened, and only 7.6 per cent of those who had children had had none of their children christened. When asked why, respondents typically gave answers in terms of what is 'normal'; much less often, some religious reason was given. Christening was seen as so automatic that only rarely was there a suggestion of pressure from kin or spouse. The commonest reason given by the few non-christeners was that the household was religiously mixed and there was uncertainty as to which church to go to.

Marriage, however, was quite different. Here the two alternatives of church and register office were recognized. 60.6 per cent of those ever married had had the church ceremony, while 39.4 per cent had used the register office. (These figures relate to latest marriages only; previous marriages are disregarded). Since christening was so automatic for most people, the relationship with age could not be usefully investigated, but a different picture emerges in the case of marriage. The relationship between age and place of marriage is shown in Table 1.13.

14

Table 1.13
Age and place of marriage

Age	Church		Elsewhere		No Answer		Total ever married	Not applicable*
	N	%	N	%	N	%	N	N
17-30	7	41.2	9	52.9	1	5.9	17	22
31-60	55	58.5	39	41.5	0	..	94	3
61 up	44	66.7	20	30.3	2	3.0	66	2
	106	59.6	68	38.8	3	1.7	177	27

* i.e., never married, no answer to whether married, or 'living as married'.

A statistically significant result is obtained if both kinds of 'no answers' are excluded, but those who were never married (or those who did not answer the question as to whether they were married) are included. The result is then highly significant (P < 0.005, x^2 = 82.8). The mean age of those who married in church is 56.5 (s = 15.2), while for the register office it is 48.4 (s = 15.6) and this difference is also highly significant (z = 3.4).

It can be seen, therefore, that there has been a slow but measurable decline in popularity of church marriage, to the point where, for the 17-30s, marriage outside church has become slightly more popular. However, the situation has never been similar to that found with christenings; the church marriage has never been automatic. None the less, comments on why church marriage was chosen suggest that Longhill people see it as 'proper', although the register office is recognized as an inferior alternative. The 'done' or 'proper' thing was to marry in church. Other reasons were given but much less often; some mentioned the Christian content of the service, while others said there had been pressures from kin, in-laws or the future spouse. Where marriage had taken place in the register office, the overwhelming reason given was financial. Less commonly, the reason was that one partner had been divorced, and some said that speed was important. There seemed to be a general consensus that the church was the 'proper' place to get married; this norm could be suspended at times of financial stringency or social disruption, but remained important. Divorce and pregnancy might also discourage church

Table 1.14
Age and preference for Christian funeral

Age	Christian funeral		No Christian funeral		Don't care		Don't know		No answer		All
	N	%	N	%	N	%	N	%	N	%	N
17-30	22	56.4	0	...	12	30.8	4	10.3	1	2.6	39
31-60	76	78.3	5	5.2	8	8.2	4	4.1	4	4.1	97
61 up	61	89.7	4	1.5	2	2.9	0	...	1	1.5	68
No answer	2	(66.7)	1	(33.3)	0	...	0	...	0	...	3
	161	77.8	10	4.8	22	10.6	8	3.9	6	2.9	207

16

marriage and the church might refuse to remarry divorcees. A few deviants did, however, express preference for the register office, and there may have been more, who were inhibited by the norm of propriety. Those who preferred the register office tended to say that they wanted to keep the wedding quiet; only two raised religious objections. Those who did not believe in God or who doubted his existence tended to go along with the norm of propriety regarding church weddings (Barker, 1978; Leonard, 1980, pp. 205-11).

The case of funerals is different again. Here respondents were asked 'When you die, would you want to have a Christian funeral?'. Respondents were therefore expressing their preferences in the knowledge that the actual decision would be made by others. Table 1.14 shows the relationship between age and form of funeral preferred.

Omitting both kinds of 'no answers', and combining those who do not want a Christian funeral with the 'don't knows', a significant difference can be observed (P < 0.005, x^2 = 17.1). Moreover, the mean age of those who wanted a Christian funeral was found to be 52.9 (s = 16.7) while that of all others who answered the question was 41.2 (s = 17.1) and this difference is also significant (z = 3.9). Thus it is demonstrated that there is a clear increase in interest in a Christian funeral as death becomes nearer, though the majority in all age-groups preferred such an arrangement. The 17-30s were most likely to be indifferent to the arrangements for such a remote event, rather than insisting upon a non-Christian funeral. It is interesting that unlike the cases of marriage and christening, religious belief did seem to make a difference here. Thus whereas 90.6 per cent of those who had said they believed in God said that they *would* want a Christian funeral, this was true of only 53.7 per cent of those who had expressed at least some doubt about God's existence. Respondents were not very articulate on reasons for having a Christian funeral. Some appealed to what is 'normal', as with christenings; though some kind of religious reason was more likely to be given for funerals than for christenings and weddings. It thus appears that death does give rise to a certain amount of thought about religious questions.

It has sometimes been noted that those who are themselves indifferent to religion none the less see the church as having some part to play in the socialization of children. Several questions were therefore included to throw light upon this matter. Respondents who had children of any age were asked whether their children attended Sunday School or had attended in the past. The results are shown in Table 1.15.

To ensure statistical significance, those who sent at least some of their children to Sunday School have to be contrasted with all the others who had children. When this is done, a highly significant relationship obtains between the respondent's age and the sending of children to Sunday School ($P < 0.005$, $x^2 = 26.7$). Moreover, the mean age of those parents who sent their children to Sunday School was 57.4 ($s = 12.3$) while for those who did not it was 42.5 ($s = 16.3$) and this difference is also highly significant ($z = 5.5$). Further questions also revealed that 60.6 per cent of respondents with children thought that Sunday School was a beneficial influence on children; those who doubted or denied the existence of God were somewhat less enthusiastic, but the difference was not statistically significant. There is, none the less, clear evidence of a slow but measurable trend away from Sunday School. This can be demonstrated even more strongly by an examination of respondents' own reports of Sunday School attendance. The question was 'When you were younger, did you go to Sunday School?', and the results appear in Table 1.16.

Table 1.15
Age and Sunday School attendance by respondents' children
(Percentages are out of total who had children)

Age (respondents)	All or some children go/went		None go/went		No answer		All with children
	N	%	N	%	N	%	N
17-30	2	11.8	13	76.5	2	11.8	17
31-60	66	71.0	22	23.7	5	5.4	93
61up	46	76.7	11	18.3	3	5.0	60
No answer	0	..	0	..	0	...	0
	114	67.1	46	27.1	10	5.9	170

Omitting both kinds of 'no answers', the difference here is statistically significant ($P < 0.005$, $x^2 = 17.1$). There is also a major difference between the mean age of those who had attended Sunday School (53.4, $s = 18.5$) and those who had not (34.0, $s = 20.8$), with $z = 4.5$. It is clear that for the over-61s (born 1925 or earlier) it would have been deviant *not* to go to Sunday School in one's youth. This

Table 1.16
Age and previous Sunday School attendance by respondent

Age	Yes, did attend		No, did not attend		No answer		All with children
	N	%	N	%	N	%	N
17-30	24	61.5	13	33.3	2	5.1	39
31-60	79	81.4	14	14.4	4	4.1	97
61up	63	92.6	3	4.4	2	2.9	68
No answer	2	(66.7)	1	(3.3)	0	...	3
	168	81.2	31	15.0	8	3.9	207

norm had declined by the time the 31-60s were growing up, though Sunday School was still very popular.[4] It remained quite popular for the 17-30s, but for them it was no longer deviant not to attend. But for those growing up on the Estate, it has now become very deviant to attend. It needs to be remembered, however, that for all respondents Sunday School only rarely led to regular adult attendance at church. For some, it terminated with confirmation, and the extent of respondents' own confirmation is shown in Table 1.17 (those with a Free Church background were asked about full membership).

Omitting the 'don't knows' and both kinds of 'no answers', the relationship can be seen to be significant ($P < 0.01$, $x^2 = 10.0$). The mean age of the confirmed was found to be 56.4 ($s = 14.9$), while for those not confirmed it was 48.6 ($s = 17.4$), and this difference is also significant ($z = 3.3$). But although there has been a marked decline in confirmation, it should be remembered that less than half are confirmed even in the oldest age-group. Thus while, as Table 1.6 shows, acceptance of a Christian designation of some kind is widespread, any stronger commitment is much less common. What seems to have happened is that in the past there was a norm of propriety with regard to confirmation, but that this has now disappeared. Respondents were not asked about confirmation of their own children, but its decline can safely be assumed given the decline in Sunday School.

Table 1.17
Age and confirmation

Age	Confirmed N	%	Not confirmed N	%	Don't know N	%	No answer N	%	All N
17-30	5	12.8	27	69.2	5	12.8	2	5.1	39
31-60	30	30.9	62	63.9	3	3.1	2	2.1	97
61 up	32	47.1	35	51.5	1	1.5	0	...	68
No answer	0	...	1	(33.3)	2	(66.7)	0	...	3
	67	32.4	125	60.4	11	5.3	4	1.9	207

Table 1.18
Age and preference for comparative or for mainly Christian RE in schools

Age	Wanted mainly Christian RE N	%	Wanted comparative RE N	%	Don't know N	%	No answer N	%	Wanted no RE N	%	All N
17-30	2	5.1	26	66.7	5	12.8	3	7.7	3	7.7	39
31-60	26	26.8	61	62.9	2	2.1	4	4.1	4	4.1	97
61 up	30	44.1	31	45.6	3	4.4	1	1.5	3	4.4	68
No answer	0	...	3	(100.0)	0	...	0	...	0	...	3
	58	28.0	121	58.5	10	4.8	8	3.9	10	4.8	207

Children also hear about religion in ordinary schools. This has always been a politically controversial subject, and respondents' attitudes were therefore examined. The issue is not about whether religion should be taught in school; 90.3 per cent wanted some form of religious education. But there can be important areas of debate as to, firstly, whether such education should be comparative or should concentrate on Christianity; and, secondly, whether the conclusion of the exercise should be that Christianity is true. The question 'Should it (religious education) be mainly about Christianity or should it compare different religions' obtained the response presented in Table 1.18.

If attention is concentrated on those who wanted mainly Christian religious education and those who wanted comparative content, and the 'no answers' for age are also omitted, the relationship with age can be seen to be statistically significant (P < 0.005, x^2 = 16.0). The difference in the mean age of those who wanted a mainly Christian content (59.3, s = 13.6) and those who wanted comparative R.E. (47.4, s = 16.9) is also significant (z = 5.0).

Respondents were also asked 'Should children be taught that Christianity is true', and the answers appear in Table 1.19.

Here the 'don't knows' are quite numerous, and can be included in a test; those who wanted no R.E. and both kinds of 'no answers' are excluded. The result is highly significant (P < 0.005, x^2 = 19.3). The mean age of those who wanted Christianity declared true was 53.9 (s = 17.1) while for those who did not want this it was 46.6 (s = 15.2). A t test reveals a significant difference (P < 0.025, t = 2.0).

The results on religious education in schools confirm what has already been reported with regard to attitudes to Christianity. Older people saw Christianity as having some form of exclusive claim, while younger people saw it more as one religion among many. The elimination of R.E. from school would not be popular with those of any age-group; but there was a strong preference in the younger age-groups for non-dogmatic and comparative teaching. Thus three-quarters of the 17-30 age-group wanted a comparative approach, while less than half of the over-61s preferred this. On the matter of declaring Christianity true, the difference was even more marked. Thus only about two-fifths of those under 31 wanted Christianity to be declared true, while nearly three-quarters of the over-61s had that expectation. Clearly, the younger favoured much more 'open' presentation of the subject, where things would not be presented as cut-and-dried; but the opposite was true of the older among Longhill people.

Table 1.19
Age and whether school RE should declare Christianity true

Age	Yes, declare true		Do not declare true		Don't know		No answer		Wanted no RE		All
	N	%	N	%	N	%	N	%	N	%	N
17-30	15	38.4	4	10.3	14	35.9	3	7.7	3	7.7	39
31-60	51	52.6	17	17.5	14	14.4	11	11.3	4	4.1	97
61 up	49	72.1	6	8.8	6	8.8	4	5.9	3	4.4	68
No answer	1	...	1	(33.3)	1	(33.3)	0	...	0	...	3
	116	56.0	28	13.5	35	16.9	18	8.7	10	4.8	207

Finally, and in view of the more voluntaristic approach to Christianity that young people seem to favour, it was thought useful to examine the question of the profile adopted by the vicar in pastoral visitation. Table 1.20 shows the relationship between approval of visiting by vicars, in relation to age. Table 1.21 relates to the question of whether vicars should do *more* visiting.

Table 1.20
Age and approval of visiting by vicars

| Age | Should visit | | Should not visit | | Don't know | | No answer | | All |
	N	%	N	%	N	%	N	%	N
17-30	21	53.8	10	25.6	6	15.4	2	5.1	39
31-60	74	76.3	13	13.4	8	8.2	2	2.1	97
61 up	49	72.1	13	19.1	5	7.4	1	1.5	68
No answer	2	(66.3)	1	(33.3)	0	..	0	..	3
	146	70.5	37	17.9	19	9.2	5	2.4	207

For Table 1.20, the relationship with age is only just statistically significant. A x^2 test concentrating only on those who gave a definite answer as to whether vicars should or should not visit, and combining the 31-60s with the over-61s, and omitting those who did not answer about their age, gives a score of $x^2 = 3.7$, just short of significance at $P < 0.05$. The differences of mean ages of the two groups also fell just short of significance at the same level. For Table 1.21, a relationship with age can be ascertained if those who favoured more visiting are contrasted with those who did not combined with those uncertain on the subject. Again, the 17-30s have to be contrasted with all the rest, and both kinds of 'no answer' are here omitted. The difference can be shown to be significant ($P <, 0.05, x^2 = 4.4$). The difference in mean ages between these two groups was not however significant.

Although the association is not particularly strong, it can be seen that there is a marked gap between the 17-30s and all those over 31 on the question of visiting by vicars. The 17-30s were less enthusiastic about visiting by vicars than were the rest, whether at the present level of activity or more than this. Over half of the 17-30s did, however, favour

Table 1.21
Age and approval of more visiting by vicars

Age	More visiting		Not more visiting		Don't know		No answer		No visiting		All	
	N	%	N	%	N	%	N	%	N	%	N	
17-30	11	28.2	3	7.7	10	25.6	3	7.7	12	30.8	39	
31-60	50	51.5	6	6.2	24	24.7	2	2.1	15	15.5	97	
61 up	38	55.9	3	4.4	7	10.3	6	8.8	14	20.6	68	
No answer	1	(33.3)	0	...	1	(33.3)	...	...	1	33.3	3	
	100	48.3	12	5.8	42	20.3	11	5.3	42	20.3	207	

24

visiting, though less than one-third wanted more. For the over-31s, by contrast, about three-quarters favoured visiting by vicars, and over one-half wanted more. Some also commented that the vicar should come only on request, except possibly in the case of the elderly and house-bound.

Vicars were seen primarily as being helpful with personal problems; about 76.8 per cent took this view. *Family* problems were the main area where vicars were seen to be useful. Bereavement was also mentioned, and problems of the elderly, ill and lonely. Social problems were much less commonly seen as matters for the vicar. A suggestion that lay visitors could be involved in similar kinds of work met with a much more lukewarm response; only 53.6 per cent favoured this idea, and 28.5 per cent were opposed.

By way of conclusion, it is worth examining the general pattern of 'religiosity' in Longhill, and then considering likely future developments, given the tendency of the young to be less religious than the old. An attempt will then be made to explain such developments.

One way of looking at the general picture is to acknowledge the fact that certain important residues of religiosity remain. Religion has for most Longhill people an important safety-net function. It is significant that remarkably few wished to put themselves beyond the pale of the church; nearly half were prepared to describe themselves as 'religious' when confronted with a choice of otherwise saying that they were not religious. Moreover, some kind of denominational preference would nearly always be forthcoming from respondents, if asked to provide this. About two-thirds believed in God. Religiously authenticated rites concerning birth, marriage and death were the norm, though in the case of marriage there was a substantial deviation from this norm. Over one-half of respondents maintained that their children went or had gone to Sunday School, and the influence of this institution was seen as salutary. Children were expected to hear about religion comparatively at school, but over half felt that the conclusion should be presentation of Christianity as true. Overwhelmingly, respondents had said that they attended church more in the past, but that mobility and the process of growing up had interefered with this. Even more said they used to go to Sunday School. Three-quarters of households had a Bible. The vicar was felt to be useful in helping with personal problems. Over half reported private prayer, and nearly half saw religion as a source of comfort and strength. Directly antagonistic attitudes to Christianity were uncommon. Even those sceptical in matters of personal belief tended to be willing to declare a denominational label and to use the church for rites of passage.

There is, however, another side to this coin. Less than half were confirmed; weekly church attendance was reported by only about one in twenty (and by comparison with actual congregations, this was obviously an exaggeration). Religiously authenticated rites of passage were performed, but much more because they were 'normal' or 'proper' than because of religious considerations. It was seen as appropriate to expose children to religious practice, but in the expectation that this would be outgrown. The church, then (and its representative, the vicar), was most commonly viewed by Longhill people as a community facility, to be used as the necessity arose; this was particularly the case for rites of passage. Christianity was also seen as part of the English heritage, into which children needed to be inducted. The church was seen as having something valuable to say on personal, especially family relationships. The vicar could help here, as a professional, but as with other professionals it was the client who was to take the initiative.

This position for the church in no way amounted to a secularist commitment, which was uncommon on Longhill. Most sceptics still saw Christianity as part of the social framework; they expected, and were expected, to perform lip-service as the necessity arose. There is no reason to suppose that sceptics were necessarily secretive about their beliefs, but it would be definitely deviant for them to let their scepticism affect such secular actions as would normally be couched in a religious framework (Leonard, 1980, p. 220, n34). It is only infrequently that the appropriate lip-service would be required, and few seem to find it irksome.

The question might be legitimately asked however as to how long this process is likely to continue. The survey of Longhill clearly shows that the younger people, especially the 17-30s, were on most items less 'religious' than their elders. They were much less likely to see themselves as 'religious', and over half of the under-31s had at least some doubt as to the existence of God. About two-fifths of them were prepared to say they were atheists or agnostics (but again, not on an official form). They were more likely to be sceptical of Christianity, though this amounts more to denial of any exclusive claims, rather than hostility. Only one-fifth saw religion as a source of comfort and strength. Only about one-quarter prayed privately as opposed to about three-fifths of their elders. They still nearly all wanted to christen their children, though there was some evidence of decline in church marriage.

The really big difference is with regard to Sunday School. The decline of the practice of sending children to Sunday School has been slow but steady. The change has been over a long period, but the big change has been with the 17-30s. Only about one-fifth of the over-61s and about one-quarter of the 31-60s did *not* send their children to Sunday School, but for the 17-30s this jumps to three-quarters. Respondents themselves were also less likely to have experienced Sunday School, the younger they were; though again the big difference is found with the 17-30s. For those over 31, it will still have been quite deviant not to attend. These results are consistent with the tendency of younger Estate dwellers to see Christianity as an option but not binding.

It is of interest that the relationship between age and adult church attendance is not very close. It must be remembered that the urban working classes have never attended church in large numbers (Inglis, 1963), and thus the survey results do not show a close relationship with age. On the matter of previous church attendance, the under-31s were less likely to report this, though they might have been including Sunday School here. For all age-groups the attitude that one outgrows church attendance seems to prevail.

There are two possible interpretations of these findings. On the one hand it could be argued that they are clear evidence of a secularization process; no matter what dimension of religiosity one takes, the young seem invariably less 'religious' than the old. On the other hand, there is the alternative explanation that religious scepticism mellows with age. Religious sympathies, it could be argued, may grow (and deviant attitudes be toned down) as people pass to the stage in the life cycle where marital and familial responsibilities are taken on. Only a study over a long period could reveal whether such is the case. But a major change that cannot be accounted for in this way is the decline in the importance of the church and religion in the socialization of children. Sunday School is no longer the norm, and religion in schools forms part of the general education process rather than being specifically concerned with the inculcation of Christianity. Those for whom the church does not have its previous role in the socialization process are likely to have a different attitude to Christianity. This does not necessarily imply an *unfavourable* attitude, but a greater awareness of alternatives means that fewer will see Christianity as having exclusive or mandatory claims. Decline in religion as a part of socialization may have implications for future contact with the church; for instance, lack of familiarity with church buildings and with the appropriate conduct within them might lead to decline in the importance of the norm of propriety regarding church marriages (Leonard, 1980, p. 211).

It cannot be too strongly emphasized that the process of change has been a gradual one. The old people on Longhill Estate were never deeply religious; nor are the young people militantly atheistic or anticlerical. There has never been more than a light veneer of religiosity in working-class communities in England, whether long-established or recently-built. Decline has been from this low level, thus few Longhill people have found the power and the position of the church to be irksome. As a consequence, few are militantly opposed to the church.

Furthermore, the process of change has been intensified for most Longhill people by the fact that they will have moved to a new area where a community has had to be developed from the beginning. Although it appears that the Estate has now developed a stable population, for the older people this will none the less stand in sharp contrast with the communities in which they themselves were socialized. A fairly large proportion of the older people on Longhill will have come from relatively close-knit working-class communities. The change in environment will have had a considerable impact upon their view of the world. Young and Willmott have documented the implications of such a change for family cohesion and consumption patterns (Young and Willmott, 1957). In the case of Hull, O'Neill has shown the difference between the culture of high-density traditional working-class housing areas and the culture of the council estate (in this case Greatfield) (O'Neill, 1981, esp. ch. 2). O'Neill found that authoritarianism was characteristic of the culture of traditional working-class areas, whereas those on the council estates in question were found to be more libertarian; moreover, their views were more consistent and they were more responsive to new ideas. Attitudes to religion did not differ very greatly, and few seemed to have any strong feelings on the subject. But the difference between the two local cultures under consideration will have important implications for people's religious attitudes.

It is true that the church has waned in its impact on the wider society generally, and not merely on relatively new estates. But there are particular problems for the church arising from the recent foundation of an estate such as Longhill. A new church such as St Margaret's, Longhill, could in its time have served as a new community facility, as a focus for reintegration. Where new norms are created some might even attend church who did not do so previously. But a much more likely reaction is that those who did attend previously could now decide to stop. No doubt many of the older people exaggerated claims regarding their activity in the past; but it is still known to be the case that a change of residence is a common reason for cessation of church attendance. Moreover, different attitudes to authority in the family on a new estate may make parental insistence upon Sunday School attendance by their children less likely. Attitudes and beliefs may be more resilient, but even here changes can be noted. The young display strong support for comparative, non-dogmatic teaching of religion in schools. This is so despite the virtual absence of non-Christian religious profession on the Estate, and the relatively young age at which full-time education has been completed. It is also of interest that, even within the Christian framework, the younger Estate dwellers were reluctant to accept firm dogmas.

As the Urban Mission Experiment got under way, the level of commitment that was expected of and obtained from the congregation of St Margaret's was high. It is significant, for instance, that the majority of the congregation attended at least one of the weekday services as well as the one held on Sunday. Also, during the mission, there was an increased emphasis on eucharistic services, and an expectation that churchgoers should also follow courses of Christian instruction.[5] The appointment of a mission priest helped in this exercise, but his stay was short-lived. He left for another parish in 1988; he felt that the mission had had some success, but he found the straints of growth too difficult to cope with for the original five-year period as originally proposed. The Estate is in a parish with a 'High Church' tradition, with a correspondingly strong emphasis on the priestly role. But in the absence of a resident priest on the Estate, *de facto* lay leadership had become firmly established and difficulties inevitably arose when clerical authority was imposed. The post of mission priest was not refilled, but the mission continued. The original aim had been for it to last until 1991, but the period was extended till 1993 so as to compensate for the experience of uncertainties and inadequate staffing. However, in 1993 not only did the mission come to an end, but St Margaret's church ceased to operate for normal Sunday religious activities. It became transformed into a charity shop selling second-hand clothing and providing cheap meals. The building is still owned by the Anglican church, and is leased by the Diocese to the charity in question. The shop is felt to perform a useful community service, which is approachable for the general public but still church-related. There are plans for cautious introduction of more overtly Christian elements. There is a proposal for a Christian Resource Centre, aiming at the provision of information about Christianity: this is to be known as 'Christian Link', and will be interdenominational. A weekly prayergroup has begun to function: its members include some who used to attend the St Margaret's Sunday services.

Among reasons for the closure of St Margaret's, competition from evangelical churches was a factor. A dwindling congregation did not prove viable in the face of short staffing and impending repairs. A House Church was formed on the Estate, by a member of St Margaret's congregation, and is now affiliated to the Evangelical Alliance. It works from rooms in a new recreation centre which was formerly a school. A few other members of the St Margaret's congregation transferred to this new body, known as 'Hope of Hull'. The Sunday service is informal, using simple and unorthodox patterns of worship which emphasize particularly the message of hope that Jesus provides for the deprived. A weeknight service is also held, aiming at those with a strong Christian commitment. There are also regular evangelical activities around this and other estates, with the church premises open most mornings for prayer.

It is also of interest that the Roman Catholic church on the Estate closed completely after Christmas 1993. Relevant factors in the closure were decreased attendance, a shortage of priests, and particularly vandalism. The Salvation Army, however, has increased its profile. The Longhill corps has now become an independent entity. There are now two Sunday adult meetings, whereas previously its premises had functioned mainly as a Sunday School (which still continues to operate).

In conclusion, it can be suggested that there has been a movement in the direction of a 'voluntary church' on Longhill Estate. Ordinary Longhill people no longer see church involvement as an appropriate part of the proper socialization of children. Yet, perhaps paradoxically, the church is still seen as part of the overall culture of English people. Any challenge to this position would be seen as deviant, and conscientious objection to occasional lip-service to Christianity would conflict with accepted norms. But so, for that matter, might be the case of active church involvement.[6] Those who continue to be religiously active are those sufficiently committed to be unaffected by secularizing trends in the wider society. The developments at St Margaret's and on the Estate generally seem therefore to confirm the suggestion by Wilson that the sectarian type is more durable in a secularized society.[7] Much research has been done upon sects which have become more like churches (Troeltsch, 1931, pp. 331-3, 338-41; Niebuhr, 1929; Wilson, 1961, 1967; Chamberlayne, 1964) but it can also be suggested that there are circumstances when a church becomes more like a sect. This process seems to have operated with St Margaret's to some extent. Anglicanism is normally regarded as representing the 'church' type. But both sect and church are logical developments of Christianity, and may be present together in a given empirical situation. Anglicanism on Longhill Estate survived for a while by becoming more like a sect, but eventually succumbed in the face of smaller bodies whose form of religious expression allowed for a higher profile for laypeople and a greater freedom in style of worship.

Such a development can be placed in the national context of decline of the larger mainstream churches and the growth of many of the smaller bodies.

This development has taken place in a situation where firm, committed views on religious matters are seen as suspect. It is unfortunate that more data were not collected on attitudes of non-churchgoers to churchpeople. For most Longhill people, it seems that religion in the form of Christianity remains a potentially unsettling force that has been successfully neutralized.

Notes

1. I am most grateful for the assistance of Fr Gordon Fisher, the Rev. Jacqueline Palmer, and Dr Adrian Worsfold, in the preparation and organization of this survey; also for subsequent assistance to Fr John Corbyn, Fr Michael Chaffey, Mr Peter Gregory, to participants in a Hull sociology seminar, and to the Hull City Council Housing Department. The survey could not have been done without the help of numerous voluntary interviewers, to whom I am most grateful.
   More details of the survey results and the earlier days of the mission can be found in *Church and People on Longhill Estate* (Forster, 1989).
2. Other evidence suggests that there is a certain bias towards the unemployed in the survey results.
3. cf. G. Ahern and G. Davie, *Inner City God*, p. 71: 'It is quite clear that a very large number of people in this country say that they believe in God but do not belong to a church as normally conceived. On the other hand, precisely these individuals when asked for information about church membership on an official form of one kind or another will respond actively rather than negatively and would not be pleased if this membership was challenged'.
4. A Gallup Poll survey reported in the *News Chronicle*, 15-17 April 1957, found 92 per cent of respondents saying that children should go to Sunday School (a higher figure than the proportion who favoured baptism (82 per cent).
5. There is a fuller discussion of the earlier days of the mission in Forster, 1989, p. 108-127.
6. cf. Ahern and Davie, *op.cit.*, p. 102: 'There was also some feeling that it was "not quite the done thing" for a man to go to church (unless perhaps a Catholic). A woman who had been in a "nerve" hospital said that the reason most people do not go to church is fear

of what the neighbours would say (others also suggested this)'. But contrast B.D. Reed (1978), where reference is made (p. 54) to 'representative oscillation', where some members of a community are reported to be reassured that others go to church 'as it were on their behalf'.

7. Wilson (1966), p. 233: 'It may be, that in response to the growing institutionalism, impersonality, and bureaucracy of modern society, religion will find new functions to perform - but that, perhaps, would be not the religion which accepts the values of the new institutionalism, the religion of ecumenism, but the religion of the sect'.

References

Ahern, G. and Davie, G. (1987), *Inner City God*, Hodder and Stoughton, London.

Barker, D.L. (1978), 'A Proper Wedding', M. Corbin (ed.), *The Couple*, Penguin, Harmondsworth, pp. 56-77.

Chamberlayne, J.H. (1964), 'From Sect to Denomination in British Methodism', *British Journal of Sociology*, XV, pp. 139-49.

Forster, P.G. (1989), *Church and People on Longhill Estate*, Hull University Department of Sociology and Social Anthropology, Hull (Occasional Paper No. 5).

Inglis, K.S. (1963), *Churches and the Working Classes in Victorian England*, Routledge, London.

Leonard, D. (1980), *Sex and Generation: A Study of Courtship and Weddings*, Tavistock, London.

Martin, D. (1965), 'Towards Eliminating the Concept of Secularization', J. Gould (ed.), *Penguin Survey of the Social Sciences*, Penguin, Harmonsworth, pp. 169-82.

Martin, D. (1967), *A Sociology of English Religion*, SCM, London.

Niebuhr, H.R. (1929), *The Social Sources of Denominationalism*, Holt, New York.

O'Neill, N. (1982), *Fascism and the Working Class*, Shakti, Southall.

Reed, B.D. (1978), *The Dynamics of Religion: Process and Movement in Christian Churches*, Darton Longman and Todd, London.

Shiner, L. (1967), 'The Meanings of Secularization', *International Yearbook for the Sociology of Religion*, 3, pp. 510-19.

Troeltsch, E. (1931), *The Social Teachings of the Christian Churches*, Macmillan, New York.

Wilson, B.R. (1961), *Sects and Society*, Heinemann, London.

Wilson, B.R. (1966), *Religion in Secular Society*, Watts, London.

Wilson, B.R. (1967), *Patterns of Sectarianism*, Heinemann, London.

Young, M.D. and Willmott, P. (1957), *Family and Kinship in East London*, Routledge, London.

2 Church evangelism and its young people

Adrian Worsfold

This study is based on my participation in and observation of an Anglican church-based teenage group in East Hull. Most of the events reported took place in the early 1980s. I had already had close contact with a Methodist group, and, having obtained some sociological training, I was interested in studying an Anglican group for comparative purposes. I disclosed my intention at the beginning of my work with the Anglican group; I was of local origin and my link with the Methodist group would have been easily discovered if I had not revealed it. From the beginning, therefore, I made public my research role, and I took notes on what I saw. However, sustained contact led me to develop a greater sociological awareness of religion which led me to postgraduate studies in that field, though these eventually had little to do with youth groups (See Worsfold, 1989). The group which is being considered here is found in an area of private housing which adjoins a much larger council estate. The minister involved in the group was evangelical in outlook, and served as a member of a team ministry where this outlook was not universally shared. However, this study will show the impact of evangelical Christianity in a small youth group whose activities were secular as well as religious. It will be suggested that evangelical Christianity maintained a high profile in such a situation, but that proposals to evangelize outsiders met with hostility even from most of the religiously committed members of the group. Thus it appears that a strong norm exists to the effect that outside display of religious commitment is to be avoided. A further point of interest will be shown to be clashes between teenagers' sexuality and the norms of conduct expected by the church.

The group, which met regularly on Sunday evenings, provided both religious and recreational activities. Initially there had been a coffee bar in the main church hall, available to anyone. This had no religious content except that an epilogue was said before closure for the night (this attracted little interest, except in one case, as will be seen). The youth club itself had 11 as the minimum age of attendance, so as to attract members of the Boys' Brigade. Most of the key actors in the present study were however in their mid-teens. The younger members (mostly boys) had separate provision made for them in respect of religious activities. For the older teenagers, there was an hour-long religious activity for those who had been confirmed (referred to here as 'religious youth'); this was followed by recreation, which began earlier for the unconfirmed (referred to here as 'non-religious youth'). Sometimes friction between the religious and the non-religious was evident during the shared recreation period. The religious tended to see themselves as the 'insiders'. Religion was part of their identity: it gave them a right to be inside the church, a place to meet that was theirs. In turn, the religious viewed the non-religious (who were much more numerous) as 'outsiders'. Recreational activities provided included skipping, 'keep fit', netball, table tennis, weightlifting, and some more cerebral pursuits The leaders saw the provision of such facilities to the non-religious as an important form of community outreach. However the males in particular sometimes engaged in disruptive activity and on one occasion noted, the minister had to be called and they were told to leave. The unruly behaviour engaged in by the non-religious was an indication that the church was not theirs. Occasionally some of the insiders also engaged in unruly behaviour but to a much lesser degree. Sexual talk and actions (e.g. dirty jokes and mild genital stimulation over clothes) were engaged in by both the religious and non-religious; but whereas the religious were concerned to ensure that such activity was not indulged in inside the church building, the outsiders had fewer such inhibitions and were on occasions ejected as a consequence.

35

The focus of this research will be mainly upon the religious youth. My concern is to examine the response to evangelical Christianity and especially to the expectation that members of the group should evangelize friends. My role was initially somewhat suspect. It was known that I was writing things down, that I had some connection with the Methodists, and that my views were agnostic and humanistic. I thus came to be seen as 'argumentative'. Initially there were attempts to exclude me from certain sessions, but rapport improved considerably with time.

Twenty people figure in the activities of the religious part of the youth group. Six of these, including the minister, could be regarded as leaders; there were then a core of seven teenagers (two male and seven female) and a periphery of six teenagers (four male and six female). Nearly all had churchgoing parents (although not always Anglican). The two who did not have churchgoing parents were one of the leaders (Gerald, age 17) and Leila (also 17). All of the girls except one attended the same single-sex secondary school outside the area. The minister was a creationist, supporting an evangelical, fundamentalist approach to Christianity. His evangelical outlook was opposed by the rector, and was not shared in the same way by others in the team ministry. He had unsuccessfully sought greater autonomy for his own church with a view to giving evangelicalism a higher profile.

Evangelism and the youth group

The evangelical approach was supported particularly strongly by Jack (age about 33), who was mostly in charge of the religious activity for those who were already confirmed. This was seen as the centre piece of the teenage group's activities. While the non-religious youth engaged in recreation, the religious youth followed a course. Jack decided that this should be based on a pamphlet *How to share Jesus with your Friends* (Smith, 1981). This used bold cartoons including teenage faces, a big fist and a motorcycle to get its message across. It was written in simple language and used the *Good News Bible*. The text began with a section 'Know what you believe', which explained that God was the 'boss', in charge of everything, but that because of the Fall people's life was unsatisfactory. This section goes on to explain that sin makes people the enemies of God, and prevents man from knowing God. However, the pamphlet continues, the remedy lies through Jesus.

Jesus is presented as being alive today, and able to change people's lives.

Particularly important for the present discussion is the section of Smith's pamphlet called 'Know how to share it'. The reader is invited to reflect upon how he or she came to know Jesus, and to think about God and the difference to life that resulted. This should be written down by the reader, who is then expected to put it in a safe place for a few days and 'go out and play football or something'. After looking at it again, the reader is expected to learn what he or she has written by heart. The account of this conversion experience is to be known as a lifeline. The reader is then asked to try to read it to a friend and elicit comments. If this proves too difficult, the pamphlet gives further advice as to how to lead into a discussion of Christian faith with friends, as follows:

After a time of general chat you might ask ...

What d'you usually do in your spare time?
I usually go out on a Friday night and play football on a Saturday.
What do you do?
Normally on a Friday I go to our church youth club.
CHURCH!
Yes. Can I tell you why?

You follow with your lifeline (Smith, 1981, p. 9).

The next step is that the evangelized teenager, if positive in response, is encouraged to pray, to meet someone who can lead him or her to Jesus, or to go to an evangelistic night. The teenager is offered a system known as A, B, C, R, which means as follows:

Admit that you are a wrong doer.
Believe everything I have told you about Jesus is true.
Count the cost of reading the Bible, going to church and of being made fun of.
Receive Jesus and the Holy Spirit with forgiveness.

The next step is to read the Good News Bible, and to attend a Christian Youth Fellowship Group.

Jack was concerned to facilitate this process by conducting 'lifeline interviews', which involved statements of personal faith and responses to the notion of evangelizing friends. Each teenager was expected to talk to Jack in a closed room. Not all, however, agreed

37

to do this. Jack regarded regular attendance for the course as very important, and provided each member with two types of card to sign. The first was to accept the faith, the second to agree to support friends.

This method met with some resistance. Judith (age 19) initially refused because she saw the interviews as an invasion of privacy, though she maintained that she did not dislike Jack personally. But the main opposition came from Leila. When the cards that members were expected to sign had been distributed, Leila threw them in, saying 'that's my decision'. Others seemed in agreement, and Leila commented that there had been a similar 'awful' course before, called *Know Jesus*. In another case, Jack's course had discouraged a potential member from attending. Around this time I discussed my involvement with the group with the minister's wife. She commented about her daughter, that she 'loved the Lord', but doubted evangelizing friends. For this reason she had decided to join the younger group instead, although she was around 14 years old.

Jack responded to the resistance at a later meeting, saying that the aim of the course was to help Christians to spread their faith to others, because this was often found difficult. He continued to take the group, but sessions based on the Smith pamphlet tended to be greeted with sullen resistance. Judith was eventually pressurized into giving an interview with Jack, and reported resentment about invasion of privacy. Leila emerged as a rebel against the idea of evangelizing friends. She was regarded as 'argumentative' by some fellow-teenagers, but she felt that argument was one of the purposes of the group. She also felt that she had a serious interest in Christianity, but was uncomfortable with what Jack put forward. She did not object to explaining about her faith to outsiders if this were asked for, but objected to being expected to do so even if people did not ask. She challenged Jack on this issue, and he replied to the effect that Christians needed help since they often gave garbled information when the opportunity arose to say something. There were more general complaints from other members of the group about lack of consultation regarding the content of meetings, and about being challenged even if they refused to say anything.

Heidi was another member of the group who expressed dissent, but the response to her was different. She was 16, and had been recruited to the group by a school friend. She tended to have moods where she debunked even some key elements of Christian doctrine. Yet it was noteworthy that Jack distinguished between her attitude and that of Leila. Whereas Jack saw Heidi as 'asking deep questions' but basically loyal, he saw Leila's open rebellion as a threat to authority. Leila eventually left the group after starting to go out with a non-religious boyfriend; but Heidi was one of the few older teenagers who remained in the group till the meetings were suspended.

These developments eventually led to a crisis meeting (I was excluded because Jack felt he could 'bawl at them better' without me). The details of what went on were not therefore observed first-hand; but it emerged that there had been much resistance to Jack, but Jack in turn thought that the course had succeeded because it had shaken people. None the less, he now spoke in terms of 'quiet Christian growth' as the appropriate strategy - a major change in orientation. He asked for topics for future meetings; one girl suggested contraception, abortion and nuclear disarmament; but these topics, of definite interest to teenagers, were rejected. Jack still supported the approach adopted in the Smith pamphlet, and maintained that no sincere Christian could oppose evangelizing. But he began to tone down the idea that the approach in the Smith pamphlet was the only appropriate method. Before long a new course began, on the subject of Revelations. This was led by Brian (age about 33). He had taken a leadership role previously, sometimes alternating with Jack. He sympathized with the evangelical approach to some extent; however, he was employed in a laboratory, and felt that as a scientist he wanted to know the 'facts'. On one occasion however this course was taken by Jack: this session seemed to frighten some people and shortly afterwards the course collapsed. It was replaced by another one on the subject of cults, and the younger people were also admitted this time. Jack was again involved in teaching this course; interest in the subject had been stimulated by an article by the minister in the Parish Magazine, which Jack said had been 'twisted' in an article in the *Hull Daily Mail*.

In the study of cults, one problem that arose was that they were viewed critically, yet some comparisons could be drawn with conversionist Christian groups. Jack was aware of this possibility, and said that, like the cult members, Christians should be totally committed. But he maintained that cults were also different since they were secretive, deceitful and evasive, sometimes 'nasty', and that they adopted unacceptable psychological pressures.

Attendances began to drop, and after the course on cults had come to an end, Brian began a new approach stressing 'Christian character'; he had a book on this subject, and this was supplemented by Bible readings. A few weeks later a six-week suspension of meetings was announced; this had been implemented because of poor attendance. Participant observation did not continue; it is understood that eventually the group was restarted but that in 1987 it succumbed to a centralization policy successfully implemented by the rector, in which worship ceased except in the main parish church. However, worship has now recommenced again in the church; there is also a 'Youth Fellowship', though this is now no longer open to outsiders because of fear of disruption.

Whoever was taking the group, the emphasis was clearly on the leader's authority. Jack was concerned to 'bawl at' the teenagers; he also rejected some discussion topics of clear interest to teenagers. Brian, for his part, saw it as inappropriate for a mere mortal to argue with God; and he also mentioned the importance of discipline and stressed the need to avoid backsliding. The teenagers themselves complained that it was 'always must', and 'they never ask us'. There was also a taboo against arguing in the group. For the leaders, religion could in no way be seen as metaphor and ritual; rather they thought in terms of a soteriology of concrete words that a credal system offers.

Thus the research demonstrates that the dominant approach that came through in the group was what Towler has described as **conversionism** (Towler, 1984, Ch. 3). This emphasizes the idea that human nature is corrupt, but that an experience of being born again is possible, leading to freedom from the weight of sin. As Towler suggests (1984, p. 39),

it is based on a real and immediate experience, rather than on a hope or an aspiration: the experience of having been set free from the weight of sin, released from a burden, and alive in an entirely new way.

There is a clear boundary drawn in conversionism between those who have and those who have not received the Spirit. The Church is the community of those who have been born again; those who are merely church members or attenders, but who have not had this experience, are excluded. At the same time, the Church as a community of believers is indispensable, since the conversionist stresses fellowship with others who are living the new life. The boundary between the earlier sinful life, and the subsequent life after accepting the Lord Jesus, is also important. It is marked by constant retelling of one's life history, showing how things changed after conversion.

40

Both these boundaries are reflected in the youth group under consideration. There was a clear distinction between the 'religious' insiders and the 'non-religious' (?sinful) outsiders; and even among the insiders, a conversion experience was necessary to qualify fully for insider status. The emphasis placed by Jack upon 'lifelines' was also consistent with the conversionist orientation of the group. Such boundaries did however make matters difficult for those who were seriously interested in Christian commitment, but who lacked the 'conversion' experience.

This approach is closely linked to, but does not automatically imply, fundamentalism. Likewise it is close to but not the same as evangelicalism. A conversion experience is important, but it can be felt in different degrees. The conversionist approach bears some similarity to sectarianism, but there is an important distinction in that for the sect the organizational boundaries are clear, whereas conversionism is compatible with a variety of denominational allegiances.

Thus for teenagers like Leila, difficulties were evident. She was the only member of the group to have crossed the line from the purely recreational 'non-religious' to the 'religious'. She had been a member of the youth group when there had been a religious epilogue, and had been attracted by this to the religious side of its activities. She was serious in her religious interests, but her Christianity was unacceptable as it stood because a subjective experience of 'conversion' was expected in order to acquire 'insider' status. Both Brian and Jack had even been known to speak of death to the unconverted. Leila was not alone in her lack of conversion experience; but those who were oriented to Christianity in this way became marginal to the church, often simply ceasing to attend the group. This did not mean that their Christianity was not serious; indeed one peripheral member of the group was intending to study theology at university and was eventually ordained.

The problem of sexuality

The Christian church has always trodden warily on the matter of support for sexual activity between the unmarried. Fundamentalists in particular have continued to regard sex between unmarried people as sinful. None the less, sin can be forgiven when admitted to be such. In the group in question, one leader (Gerald) was an unmarried father, while one eighteen year old girl (on the periphery of the group) was an unmarried mother. The question arises as to how the issue of sexual relations is handled in a group of unmarried teenagers of this kind, which is expected to profess fundamentalist Christianity. The matter was complicated by the fact that search for a fundamentalist partner could hardly be discouraged by the church. It emerges that religious motives were sometimes mixed with the aim of seeking such a partner. Thus Gerald was very interested in Leila, and maintained that his faith was close to hers; Leila, by contrast, was not interested in Gerald or in any of the group members as a potential partner. It is significant that when she met a partner from outside the group, she stopped attending. She reappeared only once, this time with her boyfriend; they came only for part of the recreational period, and then went off to see a film (Friday 13th, a semi-Satanic horror film). She did eventually continue her religious interests, but not in relation to this particular group. Gerald, by contrast, later married the daughter of a minister in an evangelical house-church elsewhere.

It is clear that while members were inside the church building, any suggestion of physical sexuality was taboo. Brian's course on Christian character was concerned to downplay the idea of 'eros' and to concentrate upon other definitions of love. Proposals to discuss abortion and contraception were rejected by Jack. Some non-religious youths were ejected by Brian for putting their hands up a girl's skirt while in the church building (the girl herself did not offer resistance). One of the religious males sometimes told risque jokes while in the church, but made sure that he was out of the leaders' earshot (but did not mind if the other religious teenagers heard). Pop music was acceptable, for the religious as well as the non-religious, and it could be harnessed for religious purposes. There was in fact a musical connection, since two members of the group had been involved in playing rock gospel music. A safe hero was Cliff Richard. He was a conversionist, part of the pop culture but also an icon of public virginity. The girls would drool over his photographs in the church, and one of them was reading his biography.

Outside the church, however, matters were somewhat different. Many of the group visited the nearby public house after the meetings, and sexual matters formed part of the conversation here and on the way home afterwards. Conversations arose on issues such as size of breasts (of the barmaid and of a member of the group), risque photographs were shown, and other sexual matters were discussed: there was also action concerning with exploring potential partners. On the walk home, females sometimes put their hands in the males' pockets to 'feel the trouser lining'. The clash between the church and sexuality was perceived but the matter was resolved by keeping the two separate. This was a matter of pride for the religious insiders, who looked down on the non-religious outsiders for their failure to observe such a taboo.

The church and the wider society

Francis (1984, p. 11) has suggested that the church tends to be less attractive to teenagers than it is to young children: and that as a consequence it is particularly interesting to look at those teenagers who do engage in some religious activity. For this reason the findings are of special interest. It is noteworthy that to a large extent recruitment to this group has been through *autogenous* growth (Currie, Gilbert and Horsley, 1977, p. 44); that is to say, the majority (all but two) had churchgoing parents. Currie and his colleagues also go on to state that the teenage period is one in which decisions are made either to join or to stop attending church (Currie, Gilbert and Horsley, 1977, pp. 90-1). There can well be a link to parental faith but also some differentiation from it, and this is found to be so with the teenagers in this study. For instance, two members of the youth group in question came from Methodist backgrounds. Francis (1984, p. 51) also shows that religious teenagers are very unenthusiastic in taking part in local evangelism: only 14 per cent of his sample were prepared to do this. Again, this finding is corroborated by the present study.

One of the intended aims of the church was outreach into the community. This reflects an Anglican concern to be some kind of guardian of the people. At the same time, some interest in religion is fostered. This is handled by associating religion with activities which are popular with teenagers and to which the church has no objection: sporting activities and pop music. This is not a new policy; as Springhall has shown (1977, p. 22; Springhall, Fraser and Hoare, 1983, p. 25), the Boys' Brigade sought to demonstrate a positive link between Christianity and activities which were popular with the age-group in question: this was by 'associating Christianity with all that was most noble and manly in a boy's sight' (Springhall, 1977, p. 22).

The link between Christianity and teenage culture is however nowadays put over in a context where religion is seen as irrelevant. Teenagers had on the whole no social reason for attending church. Some who were uninterested in religion did as has been shown participate in the secular activities of the group, but clearly rejected the religious side. If they showed any interest at all in this, it was often with the intention of engaging in disruptive behaviour. Once they attacked the symbols of the religious group, by scattering the hymn books twice in one day.

A further barrier for anyone who did show interest would in any case be the conversionist ethos of the religious activities of the group. Conversionism has difficulty in accommodating to tenuous allegiance, and presumes a much higher level of commitment. Not even all who attend church will qualify; even some of those who are ordained in the church (such as the Bishop of Durham at the time of the study) might fail to pass muster as 'Christian' by conversionist standards. Active laity, such as youth group leaders, are by contrast much more likely to be conversionist (see Towler and Coxon, 1979, p. 165, for comments on the outlook of the laity).

However, this orientation is very difficult to reconcile with outreach in the indifferent wider society. As Wilson suggests:

Those who, on the basis of a distinctive set of beliefs, hold themselves apart from the generality of people face periodic censure and contempt (Wilson, 1990, p. 26).

The leaders, especially Jack, realized this, and were concerned to prepare members of the group for such difficulties. But although membership of the group was small, even this small remnant could not be seen as attracted to the conversionist outlook. Those teenagers who showed some interest in religion wanted to see it as part of leisure and entertainment. Faith was wanted but as part of a package involving other aspects of personal relationships. It was also felt to be a mark of superior social status, especially in relation to the non-religious outsiders. The leaders, however, wanted all-or-nothing commitment. This was seen by teenagers as threatening in respect of relationships with the wider society. It involved an invasion of privacy, both of the members of the youth group and of those whom they were expected to evangelize. This could damage relationships including those with members of the opposite sex. There was no debate in the church over the rightness of the conversionist approach: the only debate was as to whether aggressive evangelism was the best way of going about this. It should be remembered that the youth group under consideration was within the Anglican church - the Established Church of England. As such it could be expected to be quite different from an organization forming part of a small sect which explicitly acknowledged that a sharp break with the wider society was expected. That the conversionist message was to dominate in a small youth group of this nature serves to emphasize that the old church/denomination/sect continuum is meaningless. The divisions lie rather within the mainstream churches, with the modern dynamic in local urban churches themselves promoting conversionism - something once thought to be particular to the sect.

References

Currie, R., Gilbert, A. and Horsley, L. (1977), *Churches and Churchgoers: Patterns of Church Growth in the British Isles since 1700*, Clarendon Press, Oxford.

Francis, L.J. (1984), *Teenagers and the Church: A Profile of Churchgoing Youth in the 1980s*, Collins, London.

Hull Daily Mail, 1, 9 April 1984.

Smith, J. (1981), *How to share Jesus with your Friends*, Pathfinders-CYFA, London.

Springhall, J. (1977), *Youth, Empire and Society: British Youth Movements 1883-1940*, Croom Helm, London.

Springhall, J., Fraser, B. and Hoare, M. (1983), *Sure and Stedfast: A History of the Boys' Brigade, 1883 to 1983*, Collins, London.

Towler, R. (1984), *The Need for Certainty: A Sociological Study of Conventional Religion*, Routledge and Kegan Paul, London.

Towler, R. and Coxon, A.P.M. (1979), *The Fate of the Anglican Clergy: A Sociological Study*, Macmillan, London.

Wilson, B.R. (1990), *The Social Dimensions of Sectarianism: Sects and New Religious Movements in Contemporary Society*, Clarendon Press, Oxford.

Worsfold, A.J. (1989), 'New Denominationalism: Tendencies towards a New Reformation of English Christianity', Hull University PhD.

3 The clergy in secular society

Christine Spencer

The secularization of society, measured by the loss of support for mainstream Christian religion, is evident in declining church attendance and membership statistics. Despite problems over the accuracy of such statistics, it is clear that the decline is continuing.[1]

As membership declines, the churches lose financial support. At the same time, upkeep of church buildings becomes ever more expensive as maintenance costs soar. The churches respond by sharing premises or by selling property, and local landmarks are lost as many churches are forced to sell their premises through lack of a sound financial base. Their congregations may be rehoused in smaller buildings, or not at all.

Remaining churches have smaller congregations and heavy financial burdens as small groups of worshippers struggle to maintain large dysfunctional buildings.

Over the past century, institutional religion has lost much influence over what are now regarded as non-religious areas of social life,[2] and if evidence of a continuing religiosity outside the church suggests that religious expression is shifting towards individual faith,[3] then the church is also losing influence over the religious areas of life.[4]

All the evidence points to traditional institutional Christianity being rejected, leaving the clergy in a somewhat unenviable position.

This calls into question the consequences of secularization for the clergy, for if secularization is interpreted as the decline of the institutional form of Christianity in favour of a developing form of personal religion (Bellah, 1965; Luckmann, 1970), then that changing expression of religion threatens the clergy if the base they work from is in decline.

A shift from the social and institutional expression of organized religion to the private sphere of individual belief indicates a shift away from a clerical interpretation of religion to one of individual understanding, which raises the question of whether even religious individuals will continue to need religious institutions and the clergy for the development and practice of their faith.

The pastoral ministry

Although the effects of secularization are felt at all levels of the church hierarchy, albeit in different ways, the problems facing the clergy are most clearly seen at the level of the local parish, where the clergy who have a pastoral ministry are at the forefront of the church and are therefore in a key position between the church and society.

Up to 1985, the total number of Christian clergy in the UK was falling, but the decline was not evenly spread throughout the denominations.[5] The denominations differ in their deployment of clergy. Fewer churches are able to support a full-time minister and often a clergyman has to take pastoral care of two, three or more churches some distance apart.[6] As churches close[7] and the catchment area for each church expands, the clergyman is called upon to serve a wider area and therefore a larger community.

Moreover, the decline in popularity of church-oriented religion is uneven. There is a decline in the popularity of public worship; church attendance for normal services has fallen.[8] Yet there is a continuing demand for religious rites of passage from those outside the church. Christenings and church weddings remain popular, and Christian funerals are the norm (Pickering, 1974, p. 63; Harrison, 1973, p. 41).

The overall result is that the clergyman is increasingly called upon to do more work for those outside the church, leaving him less time to devote to its members. As the increase in lay activity within the church continues, with the laity becoming more responsible for their church and its fellowship,[9] it would seem that non-members may have more need of the clergy than the members themselves.

Thus the uneasy position of the church in society has highlighted the question of the clergy's role, both in the church and in the wider community, and managing the balance of work between church members and the surrounding community is just one of the problems the clergy face in carrying out their role as religious functionaries within a declining institution.

These concerns formed the basis of a study of the relationship of three Hull clergyman - Anglican, Methodist and Baptist - to their church members and to the wider community.

At the time of the study, Humberside was the county with the lowest church membership in Britain (Williams, 1983), and clergy working in Hull could therefore be expected to experience the problems of the current religious situation as forcibly as clergy working in any similar urban environment.

The Anglican, Methodist and Baptist churches were chosen as three of the largest churches in England, and are all represented in the study area. Other denominations could well have been substituted, however, for denomination is not always the most significant explanatory or differentiating factor (Blaikie, 1979, p. 83). The problems facing the clergy are evident throughout the mainstream churches.

The environment of the churches

The research took place in an urban residential area of West Hull, where the churches lie in adjacent neighbourhoods which developed in the late nineteenth and early twentieth centuries but which later underwent a decline as other areas of the city became more fashionable.

In the general area of the churches, at the time of the study, empty homes and patches of waste ground could be found alongside occupied housing. All the churches suffered from the loss of population density caused by a decrease in household size and by population movement, as rebuilding schemes had cleared the older terraced housing and replaced them with small estates, housing fewer people.[10]

The churches had lost many of their original members as families moved out of the area, and they were experiencing difficulty in attracting new members from the incoming population who neither had local roots nor had had time to build up a sense of belonging to a community.

The existing churches within the area were only partly filled for normal services. During the planning stage of the redevelopment of the area, the Hull Council of Churches and the Archdeacon of the East Riding were questioned about the adequacy of churches in the area, but it was found that there was no demand for further religious facilities. It would appear then that church leaders see no expansion of the church in the area.

Research method

The research was conducted over the period of one year, between 1983 and 1984, and primarily involved a number of ministers of various denominations. Unstructured and semi-structured interviews were supplemented by observation of the minister at work within his church, through participation at church services and other events. The interviews included informal discussion which enabled the minister to speak freely on any topic felt by him to be important, and so touched on matters of concern to the clergy and not just the sociologist. As the religious specialist whom the community recognizes as a symbol of the church in society, the pastoral minister's subjective understanding and reaction to the decline in church-oriented religion is of the greatest importance in any interpretation of the current religious situation.

Owing to pressure on time and various other factors, not all the ministers in the area could be involved throughout the study. Therefore, three ministers were selected to focus the study on: an Anglican, a Methodist and a Baptist.

The problems of ministry

All three clergymen shared the well documented problems of long hours, lack of adequate leisure time and family concerns.[11] But they also suffered from problems related to their specific ministries. Rev. A (the Anglican) found that his problem was primarily one of a small and aging membership, Rev. B (the Baptist) had severe relationship problems within his church, and Rev. M (the Methodist) endured a large and stressful workload.

The clergyman and his family

The quality of a clergyman's family life can suffer because the volume of his work infringes upon his private time. Much of his work is carried out at home, and it continues into what are normally regarded as leisure hours.

With two churches to care for, a chaplaincy, circuit preaching, pastoral visitation, conducting rites of passage for the outlying community, administration, study, and attendance at church meetings, seminars and numerous other functions, Rev. M had very little time to relax and share with his family.

Rev. B's family life had been disrupted when church members had intruded on his leisure time, calling at his home without warning and outstaying their welcome. This had continued until he had put his foot down and made it painfully clear that his private life was to be respected. This had not been very popular with the church, but Rev. B pointed out that it had worked, and he now had time to share with his wife and children.

Rev. B also expressed concern over his children's education. His previous ministry had been in a very poor working class area, and although he was now living amongst a more mixed social class, it was, nonetheless, not a good area. He and his wife stressed that they were not materialists; they observed that there was much work for the church to do in underprivileged areas; but they also recognized that their children, in order to get on in life, would need a good education, and that this would be difficult to obtain in a poor area. Rev. B admitted that his occupation was low-paid, and he and his wife expressed concern that their children should not suffer because of this; so was hoping that his next ministry would be in a better area.

The length of a period of ministry is a concern shared by the clergy. Ministers of all denominations are becoming increasingly reluctant to move on because of their children's education and their wives' careers.[12] The changing social environment outside the church means that there is greater pressure on the clergy to put down roots, because the present employment situation makes it less easy for their wives to find work, and the need for children to perform well in the education system means that ministers are unwilling to uproot their families at crucial periods during their children's education.

The three Hull clergymen were no exception; all expressed a wish to be settled during their children's examination years. Rev. M considered himself lucky when he obtained his current posting, for he and his wife were already working and living locally and so he had not had to uproot his family to take up his ministry. But he hoped to avoid moving his family on until his children had completed their secondary education; Rev. A also expressed the same concern.

But the church has begun to respond to this need. The Methodist church used to post its ministers to a location for a period of three years, but presently it is five. This can be extended if the minister and church are in agreement. A ministry can therefore last for ten or even fifteen years. During the course of his ministry, Rev. M was asked to stay on for a further period, which allayed his anxieties. Rev. A was expected to stay in his parish for a minimum of five years, but longer if he so chose, and Rev. B had spent eight years in his previous church before deciding to move.

The emerging pattern for a longer ministry is preferable both for the minister and also for his church (provided it is satisfied with his work) because the church does not then have to adjust to a new ministry.

Clergy and laity

The minister's attitude to the expectations of his church, his immediate priorities, the way in which he establishes himself on his arrival and the tact with which he introduces changes have an important bearing on the future of his ministry.

When Rev. A arrived in his parish he inherited a membership of fifteen elderly ladies. His immediate priority was the survival of the church. In order to have a base to work in, he needed to keep the church open, and he recognized that changes were necessary if the church was to attract the young people it needed in order to survive. He was forced to look beyond the immediate needs of his congregation in order to bring about changes which would draw more people into the church.

He was lucky in that the fifteen original members, although used to a traditional style of worship, accepted the changes he introduced, because they shared his goals in wanting to keep the church alive. So the priorities of ministry emerged from what Rev. A felt was needed for the future of the church, not from what was or could have been expected of him from a laity used to a traditional style of worship and ministry.

The only indication that some members were not entirely happy with the changes had come in the form of mild verbal reprimands;

such as when Rev. A decided to have coffee served at the back of the church after the service, or when a new young member was caught riding a bicycle around the font. But he felt that any dissatisfaction experienced by the older members would be overcome in time. He understood that the older members had a traditional religious upbringing and that many of the new members of the church had no previous experience of the church at all. So although Rev. A felt that the original members did not really like the changes, he believed they had accepted them because they were seen to be working. He pointed out that the original members could have fought the changes, but did not do so. They accepted his suggestions because they were concerned for the future of the church.

It might be expected that a clergyman would focus his efforts on his church members. Blaikie states that most ministers centre their attention on active members of the church (Blaikie, 1979, pp. 144-7). But a lot will depend on how many members (active or otherwise) there are. In Rev. A's case, he had to extend his focus beyond the original fifteen members because there were too few of them to keep the church open for very long.

Rev. M was fortunate in that on his arrival he found that no immediate changes were necessary; the church had been well ministered. He was pleased to inherit some aspects of his predecessor's ministry, such as involvement in a social workers' luncheon club, but he also had some different interests and had gradually become involved in additional areas, which included taking on the chaplaincy of a mental hospital. So Rev. M was able to develop his own interests without having to make any radical changes. He believes that changes will occur in the evolution of church life from a response to the pressure of circumstances.

When Rev. B took up his present ministry he found a church membership of sixty to seventy people, plus a number of children and young people involved in uniformed groups. However, because he feels that Christianity can too often be neglected in the life of such groups, he would have preferred to replace them with groups under the leadership of the church, but he knew that this would have been an unpopular move, which would have been resisted. Generally, it can be seen that he met with continued resistance whenever he tried to promote his own ideas for changing and building up the church.

When a clergyman arrives in a new ministry, he is following in the footsteps of previous ministers, and the expectations that the church has of him will be shaped by their experience of those ministers.

Rev. M's predecessor had been very popular; the members continued to praise him and admitted that they had believed no other minister could be as good. But Rev. M soon came to be so well thought of that the members did not want him to leave.

It might be expected that a church which has recently experienced a problematic ministry would welcome a new minister with open arms, but this was not the case with Rev. B. When he first arrived at his church, he heard that his predecessor had experienced problems in his ministry due to ill health, and as a result the church had been allowed to run down. Rev. B now believed that the minister's problems had been caused by the church board, and that he had inherited a problematic ministry.

When placing a minister in a church, it is customary for the church to invite the prospective minister for an interview with the deacons and church committee, to see if the views and goals of the minister and church are compatible. But this failed to work for Rev. B. He complained that the members of the church board originally agreed to his ideas, but later went back on their word.

Blaikie (1979, pp. 204-5) suggests that an agreement should be signed at such a meeting by both parties. This may have helped Rev. B, but it does nothing to reflect the fellowship and trust that one would expect to find in a church.

An important factor in a church's adaptation to a new minister seems to be the length of time previous ministers have remained at the church, and for how long a period, if any, the church has been without a minister. A minister needs time to adapt to and build up a church, and a clergyman who follows a series of short stay ministers may be regarded as a transient outsider.[13]

Perhaps more problematic are the gaps between one minister's departure and the arrival of his replacement. When a church is without a minister, in order to continue to function it needs strong lay leadership, who may later be reluctant to give up the reins, or who may even feel resentment against a newcomer attempting to change 'their' church. Rev. B's church had experienced some periods without a minister and this may have contributed to the strength of the authority of some members of the church board.

Rev. M spoke of a church he knew of, which had to wait fifteen months for a new minister. He stressed that this is not expected to happen in the Methodist ministry as there is a well organized annual changeover which allows a trouble free-exchange of ministers.

53

Only one minister had severe problems with his ministry.   Rev. B complained of such severe relationship problems with his church board that he was looking for another ministry.[14]

Although he had been successful in his earlier pioneer work, Rev. B wished to avoid becoming too strongly associated with pioneer ministry, for he felt that this image would stick and would limit his career prospects.   He was aware that the problems he was experiencing in his present church might go against his chances of promotion or finding a better ministry.

Rev. M is fortunate in that he has a good relationship with his church committee and the members of his church.   The only problem he was observed to experience was the sheer bulk of his work. He admitted that the pressure could be stressful and that he felt he could not always live up to the demands of the work as well as he would like to. Yet the church was not only satisfied with his ministry, but members considered themselves extremely lucky to have him. It was generally recognized that he had a very large workload and members of the church often expressed concern about the amount of work he had to do.

Because of the high workload involved in pastoral ministry, it is impossible for the clergyman to do it all himself, or to achieve his goals for the church, without assistance from the laity.

Rev. M finds that there is far more administration than he is happy with.   This is a common complaint of the clergy.[15]   It is surprising that laymen have not been called upon to do more work in this area, but Rev. M pointed out that everything in the ministry was interwoven and that there was a need to have an overall view. He reluctantly added that some lay people are less able than others and are not capable of helping in this area.   But nonetheless he would like to see fewer administrative responsibilities for the minister, so that he could spend more time on things which he feels are more important.

The more active laity, who hold lay office in the church, tend to be the better-educated middle class church members, who often hold or have held positions of responsibility in their secular lives.[16] But this is not necessarily the case in Rev. A's church.   Many of the active laity come from the immediate locality of the church, which is a deprived working class area. Rev. A greatly encourages the local people to play an active part in the life of the church.

Rev. M and Rev. B both emphasized the need for trained laymen, particularly in the field of administration. One of Rev. B's concerns over the power wielded by the lay leadership of the church is that they are not trained.   If the churches could provide laymen with suitable and adequate training, particularly in the field of administration, the laity could better assist their ministers, who would be freer to get on with what they consider to be the key functions of their role.

The Baptist Department of Ministry has stated its intention to train laymen from the local area of the church (BUGBI, 1983, pp. 27-8). But considering the autonomy of the local Baptist church and the power invested in the laity through the church board, lay training might leave the question of the role of the ministry open unless the laymen are placed clearly under the clergy's leadership.[17]

The increasing role played by the laity raises the question of how far the layman's role should be taken, and whether there are any aspects of the clergyman's role which he regards as his sole prerogative, and which he believes the layman should not do. This consideration involves the problem of authority; it also gives insights into how the clergy are reinterpreting their role.

Rev. M emphasized the representative aspect of the minister's role, and pointed out that many people feel that unless a minister has performed a task, it has not been properly done. He feels this is particularly true with regard to the pastoral function.

This was borne out when one church member was heard to comment that they had not had a pastoral visit during Rev. M's ministry. (At the time, Rev. M had been in his ministry for approximately one year). In fact, the person had received a number of visits from lay representatives of the church, but this was not considered to be the same thing.

Although Rev. M believes that the laity give valuable assistance in pastoral visitation, preaching and conducting worship, and although he appreciates the assistance of the layman in distributing the elements (of the sacraments), he feels that the administration of the sacraments is better left to the minister, because of the minister's representative authority.

In the Baptist church this aspect of the clergyman's role is shared to a greater extent by the layman,[18] which possibly serves to undermine the authority of the Baptist clergyman, for this role is the source of the minister's symbolic and representative power.

The part played by the laity is important in enabling the minister to perform his role, but without clearly defined clergy and laity roles, there is a risk that the layman's involvement can become an intrusion into the clergyman's professional sphere, and the clergyman can feel his authority is threatened.

Rev. A's previous ministry had been in a church whose members were well educated, and who were, on his own admission, capable of a better theological argument than he was. His present church is in a working class area where he admits to feeling more comfortable because he can more freely speak to and on behalf of the people.   He believes that an important aspect of the role of a minister is that of a spokesman for those who are unable to articulate for themselves.   His previous congregation were his equals in terms of social class background; the majority had received a higher education and their theological knowledge had intruded upon his expertise.

In his present ministry the class and educational differences between himself and the laity have enabled his role interpretation of leader and spokesman to be established and maintained. So although the role of pastoral leader of the local parish is created for the Anglican minister in the structure of the church, the situation of the local parish church and the makeup of the congregation can play this aspect of his role up or down.

Yet despite each church being unique in its character and setting, many churches share the same general concerns, the most common being the dwindling size and increasing age of the congregation. All three ministers stressed the need to draw more young people into the church. They felt that the church in general needed to update its service, and make itself and its activities more relevant to the lives of people outside the church, particularly the younger generation. But at present the majority of churchgoers are older, and there is a limit to how much change can take place for the sake of a congregation that is not yet there.

Rev. A's church members realized that their church had to become more involved in the surrounding community. But the members of a church can often be more church-centred than the clergy, expecting the minister to work for them and sometimes resenting the work the clergy do for others.

When Rev. B wished to carry out a house to house visitation, in order to draw more people into the church, he found that some members of the church board were not willing to support him. A previous visitation had had a disappointing outcome (no one had responded) so it was perhaps understandable that there was little enthusiasm for a further visitation.   But Rev. B was disappointed that from a church membership of around sixty people, only a handful of members were willing to turn out to assist him.

He pointed out that only a few of the members of the church board were 'against him', but that they were strongly influential in the church. It would appear that despite the Baptist policy of shared decision making, control can lie in the hands of a few key members, with the church meeting reinforcing their power, rather than dispersing it. Rev. B believes that the majority of the church members do support him and would be willing to more actively help him if the church board would only give their approval.

However, the failure of the church members to volunteer help could be because they prefer the church to focus its efforts on its own membership rather than on a disinterested local community. Many people regard their religion as a private matter and do not wish to evangelize. And many members of the public object to overt evangelism.[19] There are also practical considerations; since the majority of church members are older people, many are not physically able to take part in evangelistic missions - Rev. A's fifteen elderly members are an example of this.

The Methodist circuit system can encourage a more open attitude to church membership (although it is not suggested here that they are any more willing to evangelize). The members of Rev. M's two churches understand that he shares his time between them, and with other churches, as he preaches throughout the circuit. They also reap the benefits of receiving visiting preachers and ministers from other churches. But they would become concerned if their own minister did not take a service for several weeks in succession because he was preaching elsewhere.

The clergyman clearly has a problem in juggling his ministerial priorities between the needs of his congregation and the needs of the wider church.

Other problems of ministry

Not only is there a decline in the size of the average church membership and congregation, but there is also a changing ratio within the congregation, between full church members and nominal members (i.e. those who do attend church but on an irregular basis[20]). This has implications both in financial terms and in the type of fellowship the church enjoys. Nominal membership and using the church for occasional worship may reduce the fellowship aspect of the church, reflecting an attitude of religious individualism. Moreover in financial terms, people who are not committed as full members are not as likely to donate on a regular basis, whether the contribution is tithed or given to the weekly collection.[21]

The local Baptist church has an affluent appearance. Its services are held in a new building, alongside which the original building is still used by several church groups whilst it is undergoing renovation. The church has sufficient funds to cover the cost, but any future expenditure will depend on the continuing support of the members and congregation. Rev. B agreed with his wife who pointed out that the church received very little financial assistance from those who attended only occasionally and donated twenty pence to the collection.

It is apparent that occasional visitors to the church will be donating to the collection only when they are there, and if indeed there is a reluctance to join the church as a full member, for whatever reason, the church will suffer financially as a result.

The Methodist church is a local landmark and has recently been renovated, but it suffers severe financial difficulties as vandalism and the high cost of maintaining such a large building make upkeep difficult. Rev. M pointed out that as the church loses its older members, many generous supporters of the church are lost.

Rev. A has overcome the financial problem, however. When he arrived in his parish, he found the church building in poor condition; some rooms were without lighting, and general repairs and renovation were necessary. He applied to the city council for a grant. The church now boasts a squash court and houses many activities organized by local people. Rev. A obtained the grant by asking for help in developing facilities with which the church could serve the community, stressing that the facilities and activities were for the community, not the church. In this way, he has more recently been successful in obtaining another large grant.

However, in the main, the church finds it increasingly difficult to finance itself. Rev. A has demonstrated that many financial difficulties can be overcome, but for most churches the day-to-day running of large dysfunctional buildings left over from the church's heyday is a continuous problem.

Some of the problems a clergyman encounters are related to specific ministries in a particular church, but there are drawbacks to working within the confines of any organization, and the potential for problems is latent within a denomination's organizational structure.

Within the Baptist church, the freedom and authority of the pastoral minister is limited. Although a minister and a church may belong to the Baptist Union (BUGBI), the autonomy of the local church and the authority of the church board is as such that the minister is employed by them, to work for them, which limits the minister's autonomy and curtails his freedom to make decisions and develop his church as he would like to. Rev. B pointed out the

Baptist church is so structured that it is difficult to make changes; the minister has no real power, and control is often in the hands of untrained laymen.

The constraints of working in a more hierarchical structure become apparent when Rev. A has to apply for special dispensation to baptize infants from another parish. The parish boundary sets a limit beyond which the minister may not freely reach, but the boundary also functions to protect the minister, for it protects his autonomy within his own parish by marking out a section of the population who are his responsibility. Without this, the workload of a clergyman could become increased and conflict between clergy of adjacent parishes could arise.

Most clergymen have a problem satisfying both the needs of the church and the needs of the surrounding community, but the Methodist clergyman is in the position of being pulled in three directions at the same time. He must consider the needs of his church, the needs of his circuit, and the needs of the local community.

Severe pressure caused Rev. M to leave the ministry some years ago. At the time he was ministering to four churches and had a huge administrative load (during one six-month period he attended 70 business meetings). Many evenings he did not arrive home until 10.30 p.m., so he saw very little of his family. He felt that he was spending too much time on administration, and was being drawn away from personal involvement with people and the things that mattered. Then a personal tragedy struck, and this, coupled with his growing concerns over his work and his family, tipped the balance in favour of him leaving the ministry. The church encouraged him to take a sector (part-time) ministry, whilst he worked in secular employment. He accepted and for a time this worked and he rapidly advanced in his new career. But once again personal tragedy struck and the pressure from his work, the church, and concern for his family, caused him to resign from the ministry.

Rev. M took up new employment, where he was promoted and able to give his family a better standard of living. But after some years he found himself becoming more involved in administration and less involved with people - the same reasons that had contributed to his leaving the ministry in the first place. He felt a growing call to return to the ministry, and after much deliberation he applied for reinstatement, knowing the shortcomings of ministry and prepared for its problems.

The Methodist minister's work of preaching for the local circuit in itself contains the potential for problems. Rev. M admitted that circuit preaching can sometimes be difficult, for it often means having to relate to people who are not known. Most of the time an immediate relationship can be established, but sometimes it may mean offering a sermon on a 'safe' but well-worn truth. And although it is possible to preach on such a 'hit and run' basis, he believes that that is a poor substitute for living alongside people, sharing the same challenges and being a more effective preacher as a result.

Rev. M feels that circuit preaching can also be a weakness pastorally, because when a visiting preacher takes a service, any strangers who attend the church do not get to meet the local minister, and the church loses the opportunity to build on this; people who could be drawn into the church are being lost because of the lack of continuity. Because his church shared its premises with an Anglican church for ten years, it is often looked to as the church of the parish, but Rev. M feels that it is not always possible to satisfy those expectations, because the circuit system prevents the minister being there all the time, as an Anglican vicar would be.

However, there are benefits to the circuit system, for circuit preaching prevents a minister from becoming rooted in his own parish. And although it is generally recognized by the minister and the congregation that some circuit preachers are better than others, the members expressed their enjoyment at receiving visiting preachers, because it allowed them to hear different interpretations of their faith.

Another benefit of the circuit system, as Rev. M pointed out, is that its member churches and its ministers enjoy a high degree of mutual support. This, to some extent, compensates for the demands on the energy and time of the Methodist clergy.

The churches of Rev. A and Rev. B belong to a local fellowship (consisting of a number of the smaller churches in the area) whose purpose is to enjoy shared worship and to work together on evangelistic missions (although a source of disappointment for Rev. B was his church's reluctance to take part in a recent evangelical campaign).[22] The fellowship meets only very occasionally for special services, such as at Easter and Christmas. For the rest of the time the member churches function individually. The relationship is token rather than functional.

In considering the difficulties of ministry it is worth questioning whether the selection procedures of the churches attract suitable candidates, and whether the training the churches provide for their ministers is adequate for the realities of ministry.

The selection procedure for ministerial candidates for the Methodist Church is an extended process which can take up to six years. The Baptist Church, however, specifies a minimum of only one year before an applicant can be accepted for its ministry, although Rev. B's application for ministry was accepted after seven months.

Although candidates for the Baptist ministry are generally required to have university entrance qualifications for entry to Baptist Theological Colleges, the Baptist Church recognizes that many candidates without formal qualifications are called to the ministry. For these candidates, the Baptist Church provides in-service training.[23] This was the case for Rev. B.

Some years previously, as a Bible College student, Rev. B had gained experience of preaching and had later worked in several Christian youth centres. He had also spent a year assisting a church minister. When he was given the ministry of a Baptist church, he felt that he had been thrown in at the deep end and left to get on with it.

His first ministry was classed as a pioneer ministry. Although strictly speaking a pioneer ministry is in a new church, the church Rev. B was sent to had been without a minister for several yeas, and was so run down that it needed re-establishing. After facing and successfully overcoming some severe obstacles, Rev. B built up the church and established several successful youth groups. But after a time, the groups floundered. Yet despite this, he regarded his first ministry as being a success, for as a pioneer minister he had been able to develop and put into practice his own ideas.

This had led him to expect the same kind of freedom in his present position, but he found himself ministering to an established church which needed different handling. Rev. B was confident that he had the ability to identify and solve the church's problems, but his biggest stumbling block was the church board. The members of the committee did not agree to his ideas, and their attitude became the biggest problem that Rev. B faced. He found the pattern of church life was already well established and the church was resistant to change; he felt unprepared for the situation he found himself in, and complained that he had not been given any real training. He now stressed his wish to attend a theological college.

Rev. M had attended a theological college, but felt that no amount of training could prepare a clergyman for his work, which is constantly changing and developing. He considered that the theological training he had received was excellent, although the pastoral side of training had been somewhat lacking, for it concentrated on the organizational side of the work leaving the spiritual side neglected. He felt that it was important to understand that pastoral work differs from social work, and that training involved discovering how it differs. But Rev. M emphasized that training for the ministry was a continuous process taking place in the ongoing context of ministry; and that a minister learnt from the situation he worked in.

Rev. B feels that a theological college would provide him with the training he lacked. He pointed out that his predecessor at his present church had also lacked any real training. Yet, despite being a very experienced minister, he had also suffered a problematic ministry. Rev. B therefore felt that experience was not a substitute for training. This raises the question of whether the Baptist Church adequately prepares its clergymen for their ministry, or whether Rev. B lacked a realistic assessment over what could be achieved in his present ministry.

Every parish clergyman will have goals for the ministry of his church. These may be long term aims, but ministerial priorities usually emerge from more immediate necessities: the solving of problems which stand in the way of progress toward goal achievement, or difficulties that must be overcome to give the church a firm foundation on which to build.

A minister's priorities arise from what he feels is needed in a situation and not necessarily from what is expected of him. But judgement of those needs is dependent upon his experience, and his approach is biased by his attitude. Moreover, a clergyman will also develop his own ministerial style. But a ministerial style is not necessarily a package that can be successfully carried around from one church to another.

Rev. A and Rev. B both found that their priorities did not match their churches' expectations of them as pastoral ministers - Rev. A's laity expected a traditional style of leadership, Rev. B's church expected him to do their bidding. Rev. A was lucky in that his style of leadership suited his present church and also in that he was able to convince the laity that his priorities matched the church's needs. Rev. B was less fortunate - the problems he identified in the life of the church could not be solved without his first solving the relationship problem. He had expected to take on the same leadership role which he had previously enjoyed and wanted to bring his own style of ministry to the church rather than just provide what was expected of him. But ministry, like the church, needs to be adaptive.

Each minister has a leaning toward his own 'ideal' ministry, but as Rev. M pointed out, the ideal and the real can be quite different. Ministry is often a compromise. If a minister is lucky, the laity can help bridge the gap between an ideal and a real ministry.

Rev. B expressed the wish to have a preaching and teaching ministry, and he had come to his present church believing that he would have the teaching ministry he desired. The reality was disappointing; he expected the laity to act on his ideas and give him assistance in carrying out his evangelistic plans for the church, which would leave him free to take pastoral care and to teach, but he found that he was expected to do everything else as well. For Rev. B, the gap between ideal and real became too wide.

A minister's 'ideal' ministry reflects his beliefs and attitudes. Both Rev. B and Rev. A are absolutist in their theology. Rev. B does not agree with the Baptist Union's position on the subject of female ministers, which he feels is contrary to scripture. He places heavy stress on the word of the Bible (which, perhaps, reflects his Bible College training), but his absolutist stance may reflect a reluctance to adjust his ideal.

Rev. A also believes in the literal truth of the Bible. He does not hold with the more radical theologies, such as the Bishop of Durham's well publicized comments on the Bible as symbolic truth.[24] Like Rev. B, he sees himself as a leader of his church, and he feels comfortable with his present church because his self image of spokesman is not being challenged.

Rev. M's ideal, however, is not that of a leader, but an enabler. He is not an absolutist; he pointed out that the Bible's value is in the overall truth it holds. This stance allows for other interpretations to exist and for a sharing of knowledge with his congregation, whom he sees as fellow travellers on a spiritual path. He believes that ministry is an interactive process, and admits that he is not in the position of knowing it all, and that his ministry is one of questioning and continuous learning.

A parish clergyman must of necessity identify the needs of his church and set goals for his ministry. He will have to overcome any problems inherent in the ministry, or which may arise in the course of his ministry, in order to achieve his goals; but in turn, his goals may need to be adapted to take account of whatever problems his ministry faces.

The length of a period of ministry is an important consideration when establishing goals, for there is a minimum time considered necessary in order to fulfil the goals of a ministry.

At the onset of the study, Rev. A had spent five years in his parish. He had already tackled the major problems he faced in his ministry: - in particular a low membership rate and the financial expense of renovation. It had taken him three years to begin to make headway, and only after five years was he seeing results. He estimated that it would take another five for the church to escalate.

After three years in his present position, Rev. B still considered himself a newcomer, and had not yet been able to see any progress. He pointed out that in his previous position, it had taken five years to lay the foundations for building up his church.

Rev. M had different goals for his two churches. The church which lay in the study area was well established, but his second church (which had been disrupted somewhat whilst a new church building was erected) had yet to be linked to its surrounding community, a process which would take time. But during the course of the study, Rev. M had his period of ministry extended.

The longer periods of ministry which are indicated for the future offer more opportunity for a community-focused ministry to develop, and it would appear that the Baptist and Methodist church may be shifting their style of ministry towards the more permanent Anglican model.

Church and the wider society

In looking at the minister's role in the church and the wider community, it is necessary to understand who the minister is primarily working for. The denominational context is important here.

The Anglican minister has his parish set out for him. Although Rev. A is aware that the majority of people in his parish will never attend his church on a regular basis, he nonetheless sees his work as being for the whole community. His use of the church as a base for community activity reflects this.

The Methodist minister works for his church or churches and for the local circuit, and he is also there for any members of the surrounding community who need his services.

But the Baptist church has a much vaguer concept of community, for although the church is there to serve its local community, it stresses that it is a church for believers. This was reflected in Rev. B's attitude to catering for those outside the church - he admitted that there was a limit to how much help he was willing to give to those outside the Baptist church. The Baptist church emphasized the need to belong to the church as a full and committed member. Nominal membership alone is not enough; it is possible to be a Christian without belonging to a church, but it is not possible to be a Baptist without belonging to a church (Beasley-Murray, n.d.b.). So although in theory the Baptist clergyman is there to serve the surrounding community, in practice he works for his church.

Rev. B was concerned because he felt that his church did not serve the surrounding community. He felt that for the church to meet the community on any level of understanding would take commitment, and pointed out that churches, as well as individual members, were at different levels of commitment. Some members wanted to go to church and do nothing else. His plans to evangelize had not been supported. He pointed out that the only involvement his church had with the local community was with the uniformed children's groups in which Christianity played only a peripheral role.

It would appear then, that in practice the Baptist minister works for his church, which is focused toward its own community of believers; and this suggests that the Baptist church functions primarily for itself, whereas the Anglican and the Methodist churches tend to put more stress on the surrounding community. There is, therefore, a potentially higher workload for the Anglican and Methodist minister.

The minister's focus will therefore be drawn to a greater or lesser extent toward serving the community of believers inside the church, or serving the community outside the church, with the church acting as a base to work from.

The individual minister's attitude varies as to whether those outside the church are to be helped where they are, or whether they must first be brought into the church.

Rev. B was eager for his church to evangelize the local community to draw more members into the church, but he was reluctant to work for those outside the church who chose to remain outside of it. Rev. A did not appear to differentiate between work for committed members of the church and for members of the community at large; he stressed that he was there for all the people in his parish. Rev. M also had a strong community focus. As mentioned above, partly because of its previous sharing arrangement, Rev. M's church tends to be seen by the surrounding community as the parish church for that area, which enables him to put his outward focus into practice. The Methodist circuit system also encourages the minister to look beyond his immediate church and its surroundings.

It can be seen that the clergyman's focus largely follows from his church's organization; the Baptist minister is (in practice, if not in theory) employed to work for his particular church, whereas the Anglican minister is placed in his church to serve his parish.

As the number of churches and ministers decreases, each clergyman becomes responsible for acting on behalf of a greater number of people outside the church, whether this takes the form of pastoral visitation or conducting rites of passage. This increases the clergyman's workload, but it also provides him with an opportunity for contact with people he would not otherwise meet. Despite the extra work involved, both Rev. A and Rev. M emphasize the positive side to this contact.

Many people outside the church still ask for a baptism service for their infants. Rev. X, whose Anglican parish is adjacent to that of Rev. A, refuses this service if the parents are not members of his church.[25] He offers a blessing instead, but many people are not content with this, and will shop around for a church which will serve their needs. This sometimes results in the parents approaching Rev. A, but he is not allowed to go ahead without special dispensation.

Rev. A was eager to point out that he is happy to baptize infants from his own parish. One of the changes he made, when he arrived in his ministry, was to bring the baptism service into the normal church service, to give the parents contact with the church. He believes that the demand for baptism comes from an underlying folk religion, and explained that many people who do not attend church are nonetheless religious. But the matter of baptisms for those residing outside his parish is taken out of his hands.

Rev. M receives a lot of requests for baptisms from parents who live in the parish of Rev. X. This does not create any friction between the churches, as Rev. M explained that if there is no relationship between the churches involved, it creates no problems, and there is no relationship between his church and Rev. X's. Although ideally Rev. M would like to baptize infants within the normal church service, sometimes he has so many infants to baptize (on some occasions as many as six) that he has to hold a special baptism service in the afternoon. But he feels that baptisms create a valuable contact with those outside the church.

It could be that ministers who refuse such rites of passage to non-churchgoers are cutting their own throats, for although such fleeting contacts rarely draw people into church membership. Rev. M points out that that is not his aim. He considers that such contact plays a part in maintaining religious interest outside the church.

Rev. B, as a Baptist, does not have the problem of infant baptism, but is asked to conduct wedding services for members of the community. He will do this if they are willing to accept Baptist instruction. He also finds that people outside the church turn to him for pastoral help. He pointed out that he has given such help in the past, and was willing to do so in the future, but that there was a limit to how much time he was willing to spend working for those outside the church.

Rev. M spends a great deal of his pastoral visitation time on people who are outside of the church. But after one year in his ministry, he had not made pastoral visits to all the members of his churches. And although the church members often expressed pleasure at seeing infants from the surrounding community baptized during the normal service, occasionally someone would point out that the parents were not church members and would not come back.

A minister who spends time on those outside the church will have less time to spend on church members. Rev. M attends approximately 100 funerals a year, of which only a handful are for members of his church. During one interview, he explained that he had attended six funerals that week, and on each occasion had also visited the bereaved. This had obviously been a daunting process. But he stressed the positive side of the situation, that it brought him into contact with people he would not otherwise meet. And he believes that without this contact the minister is in danger of identifying religion solely with church-going.

Rev. A has now built up his church from a membership of fifteen to between forty and fifty members. He is proud of the fact that the majority of the members of his church come from the local community, and spoke of other churches which had to rely on a mainly imported congregation. He stated that he could have built the church up in the same way, but did not want to do so. He wanted his members and the people who use the church to come from the surrounding area, because in that way he had a church which served the community.

He has also established contact with the local community in other ways; by including advertisements in the church magazine he has contacts with many local businesses. The magazine carries approximately forty advertisements, plus a long list of sponsors. This has been a successful venture, both in terms of establishing links and in terms of income. As well as church groups and uniformed children's organizations, the church also houses many clubs and activities as diverse as dancing, karate and badminton, which are run by and for members of the local community.

The image that people hold of the clergyman will influence their expectations of him in his ministerial role.

Rev. M believes that amongst churchgoers, the image of the clergyman and therefore what people expect from him is based on their experience of himself and other ministers they have had contact with. But he considers that the image of the clergy held by the world at large, is often based on very limited experience, or none at all. He considers that the image of the clergy is something of a problem.

He pointed out that people often think of the clergyman as a nice old-fashioned chap, but Rev. M has seen examples of bitterness between individuals in the church which causes him concern with regard to the church's image to the world. Because he works for a circuit he is made aware of the image of other clergy, and feels there is often too much unctuousness and pompousness about the clergy. He believes that formal teaching and worship do not necessarily help to convey Christianity, and that a minister should also be a recognizable human being. He pointed out that sanctity is a special quality, seen in human beings who are good in a radiant way, but that there are not a lot of these about, in the church or anywhere else.

Rev. M explained that the image of the minister is tied up with the image of the church in general, but as he works for two churches and the circuit, he does not think he is identified with the local area as a vicar would be. Although a Methodist church, because of its situational position, can function like a parish church (and to a certain extent his does) he points out that if it were not for the fact that he conducts rites of passage, the majority living in the community would not know him. But he hopes that people who have had contact with him will see the minister and his church as being open to and for them.

Rev. A believes that the image and status of the clergyman is relative to the situation he works in. He began his ministerial career as a curate in an affluent suburban area, where he was relatively poor. But in his present ministry, living in a large vicarage in a poor area, he is considered wealthy, yet his income is only marginally higher than it was previously.

Rev. A was pleased to point out that he did not think he fitted the stereotyped Anglican vicar image, because although he came from a rural middle class background, he had failed his 11-plus and so had not received the middle class education typical of most Anglican vicars. But he nonetheless identifies with his role in the Anglican tradition of paternalism. His experience in his present church has reinforced that ideal; the church's willingness to give him a free hand in the running of the parish has enabled his self-image as leader and spokesman to be maintained.

Rev. B was deeply concerned over the image of the clergy, and had a fear of sharing what he regarded as an effeminate image. His first ministry had been in Scotland, where as a minister he had enjoyed great respect - even non-churchgoers would invite him into their homes. But during house to house visitations in the area surrounding his present church, he met a disinterested population. He found it hard to accept that people did not invite him into their homes, and complained that if a couple answered the door, the man would not discuss religion with him but would go inside, leaving the wife to do the talking. Rev. B spoke disparagingly of the clergy who wear 'little dresses', which he feels is damaging to the image of the ministry; and he has given up wearing the dog collar because he believes it is a symbol of an outdated ministry, and through discarding it he hopes to avoid being associated with the traditional image of the ministry.

Indeed, on a first observation visit to Rev. B's church, not having met Rev. B beforehand, it was not immediately apparent who the minister of the church was. Perhaps in rejecting the clerical image and removing the visual distinction between himself and the layman, Rev. B has contributed to undermining his ministerial authority.

Despite the community's use of the church for rites of passage, the majority of the population continue to shy away from regular contact with the church.

There are many reasons why people stay away from the church; some of these are external to the church, some are internal, and some lie in the relationship between the church and the world.

Rev. A spoke of some of the external reasons why people do not attend church. For example, practical reasons such as whether people have a young family. For this reason he has introduced a creche for the infants of parents who wish to attend services. Although he admits that this can be a bit noisy, it overcomes one of the problems of parents who might otherwise stay away.

Rev. A believes that many people are deterred from attending the church because of the church's activities, such as hymn singing, rather than by a lack of religious conviction. Rev. M expressed a similar view. He explained that many church activities did not appeal to or have any real meaning for those outside the church.

There are also problems in society which make acceptance of the church difficult. Rev. M believes that materialism is such a problem, because many people use material substitutes to give deeper meaning to life. He explained that people who do not have a religion put something else in its place to invest with value, such as relationships or careers, and are often concerned only with improving their life style, living cocooned from reality unless a sudden intrusion, such as a death, occurs. He believes that people do care for their family and friends, but that there is a need to be concerned about the whole of humanity.

Rev. M considers one of the biggest problems facing the church today to be the problem of credibility, i.e. how closely a person's life represents his or her faith. He believes that the church's credibility is damaged if there is a gap between what people in the church say life should be, and how they act.

He also pointed to the problem of relevance - that the church does not always speak to people's conditions and so is not relevant to everybody.

He explained that the clergy as a whole are attempting to find a different language to re-present the Christian message; but that it is necessary to find a symbol or concept which represents the same reality as that which is being replaced, otherwise the meaning of the message is changed. He stresses that it is a long term project.

With regard to the clergy's problem in relating to people outside of the church, it was noted that both Rev. A and Rev. B shared the habit of interpreting everything in terms of religion. For example, with regard to financial problems there was a distinct 'God Will Provide' attitude, and although Rev. A coupled this with sound financial sense, nonetheless people outside of the church do not relate to this language or speak in the same terms. There is a need to make the language of the church more relevant to society, as Rev. M suggests, in order for conversation to take place.

The changes that Rev. A has introduced have largely taken place within his church, making its services more relevant and its facilities available to the surrounding community. But although Rev. A promotes the activities of the church, its membership could not take the church to the community with evangelistic missions; it was necessary to establish the church as the focal point for members of the community to come to. Thus Rev. A's church functions in the traditional Anglican mould; he is trying to escape from the traditional style of church worship within the traditional structure of the Anglican church.

As the study came to a close, Rev. A, after having established a firm base for his church, was concerned to see it grow, a sentiment no doubt shared by most clergymen.

Because he spent most of his time working for the study area church, Rev. M's immediate priority was to establish links between his new church and its community. He believes the study area church already functions as a community church.

In more general terms, Rev. M would like to see more people at worship in his churches, but, more than that, he would like to see more people accept Christian values in their everyday lives. He spoke of how it was possible to build a boundary between the church and the world by creating a sect-like church; but he does not want to see such boundaries drawn, for he believes that God is not concerned with church life as such, but with the whole range of human activity. He thinks the church should reflect that diversity and be concerned with the community around and outside of itself.

Some of Rev. B's concerns were for his career. He felt that he could not progress any further at his present church because he needed more authority, but in order for a minister to gain authority there would first need to be changes in the structure of the Baptist Church. Rev. B felt that when he moved on, any minister following him would face the same problems and he feared that his church might close at some time in the future.

Rev. B would like a teaching ministry. During his present ministry he has worked hard for and gained an Open University degree: but he stressed that he still wished to attend a theological college, for he believed that this would furnish him with the training he felt he lacked, and would better enable him to teach and lead others.

The decline of mainstream Christianity has made the Church sit up and take stock, and the numerical decline may herald in a new style of worship, allowing an interactive participation which was not possible with the large congregations of the past.

The clergy see the adaptation of the church to a changing society as a challenging rather than a daunting process. In attempting to make that adaptation, the clergy are having to rethink their style of ministry.

Rev. B has expressed the desire to take his ministry into society, into pubs and clubs, in order to reach the people who will not attend a church. He feels that the church is outdated and bogged down in tradition, and needs to keep pace with the world at large.

Rev. A has taken on the unlikely role of chaplain of a rugby club. He pointed out that as unemployment continues to rise, the leisure industries offer a growing opportunity for contact with those outside the church.

The membership of the majority of churches have become fixed in conservative and traditional patterns of worship. But the church's financial crisis might yet become a blessing.

Rev. M is now prepared for the selling of his church; its financial problems have become too great. Despite regrets about the loss of a fine building, he feels that a smaller building would facilitate new methods of worship where the minister could come down from the pulpit enabling minister and layman to engage in a more dialectic process of sharing faith.

The individual in society may be responsible for his or her own religious development, but Rev. M feels that the church building is necessary as a place for people to meet, and to provide a focus for community religion. Individuals would then be able to develop their faith using the church and its minister as a valuable resource for personal and communal growth.

There is a wealth of spiritual interest outside the church, and if the church can tap this source there is plenty of scope for the ministry of the future.

The future of the ministry

None of the ministers interviewed expressed concern with regard to their personal future in the ministry. All three felt confident and secure in their calling and wanted to remain in pastoral ministry, although Rev. B was becoming increasingly interested in teaching trainees for the ministry. He saw this as one way of having the teaching ministry he desired, without lay interference. However, it is unlikely that he will be able to achieve this until he has gained more experience, for he would need to learn how to overcome ministerial problems in order to better advise others. But despite his history of troubles, he still felt that the Baptist church offered great opportunity and he did not doubt that his future remained with the Baptist church.

Rev. M, despite his earlier suscess in secular career, did not have any regrets about returning to the ministry.

Rev. A felt that he might consider, in about ten years' time, that he had done all he could in his present ministry, or he might choose to stay on. He knew that he could stay in his parish until his retirement.

Perhaps part of the reason for the clergymen's confidence is that it is hard to believe your job is becoming redundant whilst you are being run off your feet.

(Since the study was completed, Rev. B has moved on and now has a pastoral ministry in another city. Rev. A remains in his parish. And Rev. M, after taking a short rest, returned to his ministry before spending some months working on a church research project at a university. He returned to his ministry for a further period before moving on to a new posting in a nearby circuit. His study area church was put under the care of another minister, but its longstanding financial problems have finally taken their toll and the church will close in the near future. The congregation will be dispersed as members move to other churches).

Since the completion of this study the Baptist church nationally has greatly increased its numbers of clergymen. It is ironical that a church with such strong lay activity and power has expanded the ranks of the clergy, particularly as membership of the Baptist church in England is relatively stable (Brierley and Longley, 1991, p. 214). It is likely that deployment of an expanded ministry is part of an overall effort by the Baptist church to take advantage of the growth of the smaller churches, and it could be that a stronger concept of ministry will emerge as a result.

It seems for the moment that the decline in the ranks of the Anglican clergy has been stabilized, although members continue to fall away at an alarming rate (Brierley and Longley, 1991, p. 214).

For Methodists, the loss of membership continues but at a slower rate than previously; ministers continue to be lost, but the most serious decline is in the number of churches (Brierley and Longley, 1991, p. 214).

The overall position of the mainstream Christian churches continues to look unhealthy. And despite the fact that the pastoral clergyman is now responsible for the pastoral care of fewer church members (Brierley and Longley, 1991, p. 27) so far the loss of churches has not made any significant difference in reducing the number of churches a minister is responsible for. The ministry of two or more churches, with a corresponding increase in administrative work, or the care of a larger parish with the problems of ministering to a more widespread community, have brought about a paradoxical situation where the clergy are overburdened whilst the church they service is in decline.

Notes

1. For a brief discussion of the problem of obtaining accurate statistics, see Brierley, 1986, p. 7. Recent statistics showing continuing decline can be found in Brierley and Longley, 1991, pp. 210, 212-5.
2. See, for instance, Wilson, 1966, pp. 56-8.
3. For evidence of a spiritual interest outside the church see, for instance, surveys on 'para-normal behaviour' in Gallup (ed.), 1976, Vol. 2 [1965-75], pp. 1282-3, 1417-18.
4. See, for instance, Bellah, 1965.
5. For decline in numbers of clergy (by denomination) see Brierley, 1986, p. 132.
6. Brierley, 1988, p. 13. Brierley states that a minister may be responsible for as many as eight churches.
7. For statistics on the declining number of churches, see Brierley, 1986, p. 132.
8. Church membership statistics are based on attendance at public worship. See Brierley, 1991, p. 210.
9. For the general argument that the laity are exercising more control over their church, see Cantrell, Krile and Donohue, 1983.
10. Hull City Council Planning Department, personal communication.
11. See, for example, Blaikie, 1979, pp. 161-5, 183-7.
12. 'Comment: Are Ministers becoming too Choosy?', *Baptist Times*, 24 May 1984, p. 2.
13. See Clark, 1970, esp. pp. 52-3. Although Clark's discussion of laity strength and the transient character of the Methodist ministry does not refer to the Baptist church, his findings have a general significance, and he fully discusses leadership strength and length of ministry.
14. BUGBI (1983), p. 8 describes a scenario very similar to that experienced by Rev. B., and predicts that in such a situation, the minister will move on.
15. Blizzard (1957) conducted research on how much time the average clergyman spent on various aspects of his role. Administration was found to be the most time-consuming task. Ranson, Bryman and Hinings (1977, p. 64) found out that the clergy generally dislike the administrative and organizational aspects of their role, which take up considerable time and distract attention from other aspects of their work. Blaikie (1979, pp. 167-9, 172-5) states that the clergy's

organizational work is time-consuming and gives little satisfaction.

16. Burton (1974) points out that although the social class composition of a church depends upon its location, the lay leadership tends to come from among the higher social classes: often those who commute from outside the area.

17. BUGBI have produced some useful sets of leaflets explaining how the Baptist church functions (Baptist Basics Series, and Baptist Heritage Series). Of particular interest are Beasley-Murray (n.d.b.), Hayden (n.d.) and Quicke (n.d.).

18. The role of the church deacon is discussed by Wortley (n.d.), and Beasley-Murray (n.d.a.).

19. The common reaction to the door to door witnessing of the Mormon church and Jehovah's Witnesses is an example of this.

20. Brierley (1986, p. 11) believes that there is a trend towards fewer nominal members, so that churchgoing will become more of a commitment for fewer people.

21. Brierley (1988, p. 16) states that although it is not known who gives the most money to the church, it is unlikely that non-members give more than members.

22. Billy Graham Mission England Campaign, 1984.

23. See the pamphlet 'Entering the Baptist Ministry' (BUGBI, n.d.).

24. For example, the comment made by the Bishop of Durham, Dr. David Jenkins, on 'Inner Space' (Tyne Tees Television Broadcast on Easter Day, 1989) to the effect that the Resurrection was spiritual (rather than physical).

25. A letter written by a parishioner to a local newspaper was given the caption 'One baptism in six years - in parish of St John the Baptist!'. See 'Viewpoints', readers' letters page in *Hull Daily Mail*, 23 August 1983, p. 9. Rev. X responded by pointing out that he offers a blessing instead: 'God getting his message across', in 'Viewpoints', *Hull Daily Mail*, 27 August, 1983.

References

Baptist Times, 24 May 1984.

Beasley-Murray, P. (n.d.a.), *The Ministry of Deacons*, BUGBI, London.

Beasley-Murray, P. (n.d.b.), *Why Baptism and Church Membership?*, BUGBI, London.

Bellah, R. (1965), 'Religious Evolution', in Lessa, W.A. and Vogt, E.Z., *Reader in Comparative Religion: An Anthropological Approach*, Harper and Row, New York.

Blaikie, N.W.H. (1979), *The Plight of the Australian Clergy: to convert, care or challenge?*, University of Queensland Press, St. Lucia.

Blizzard, S. (1957), 'The Minister's Dilemma', *Christian Century*, Vol. 73, No. 17, (23 April).

Brierley, P. (ed.) (1986), *UK Christian Handbook 1987/88*, MARC Europe, Bromley.

Brierley, P. (ed.) (1988), *UK Christian Handbook 1989/80*, MARC Europe, Bromley.

Brierley, P. and Longley, D. (1991), *UK Christian Handbook 1992/93*, MARC Europe, Bromley.

BUGBI (n.d.), *Entering the Baptist Ministry*, London.

BUGBI (1983), *Half the Denomination: The Report of the Working Group on the Care of Small Churches*, London.

Burton, L. (1974), 'Social Class in the Local Church: A Study of Two Methodist Churches in the Midlands', *Sociological Yearbook of Religion in Britain*, 8, pp. 15-29.

Cantrell, R.F., Krile, J.F. and Donohue, G.A. (1983), 'Parish Autonomy: Measuring Denominational Differences', *Journal for the Scientific Study of Religion*, 22, pp. 276-87.

Clark, D.B. (1970), 'Local and Cosmopolitan Aspects of Religious Activity in a Northern Suburb', *Sociological Yearbook of Religion in Britain*, 3, pp. 45-63.

Gallup, G. (ed.) (1976), *Gallup International Public Opinion Polls: Great Britain 1937-1975*, 2 vols., Greenwood Press, Westport, Connecticut.

Harrison, K.K. (1973), 'The Decline of Methodism in Kingston upon Hull in the Twentieth Century', Hull University M.A.

Hayden, R. (n.d.), 'The Church Meeting - what is it?', BUGBI, London.

Hull Daily Mail, 23 August 1983, 27 August 1983.

Kingston upon Hull City Planning Office (1981), *Newington District Plan: Draft Proposals*, Hull.

Luckmann, T. ([1967] 1970), *The Invisible Religion: The Problem of Religion in Modern Society*, Macmillan, New York.

Pickering, W.S.F. (1974), 'The Persistence of Rites of Passage', *British Journal of Sociology*, 25, pp. 63-78.

Quicke, M. (n.d.), *Baptist Beliefs*, BUGBI, London.

Ranson, S., Bryman, A. and Hinings, B. (1977), *Clergy, Ministers and Priests*, Routledge and Kegan Paul, London.

Williams, M. (ed.) (1983), 'Society Today: Religion', *New Society*, 63. 1061, 17 MARCh 1983 (supplement pp. i-iv).

Wilson, B.R. (1966), *Religion in Secular Society: A Sociological Comment*, Watts, London.

Wortley, P. (n.d.), *What is a Baptist Church?*, BUGBI, London.

4 Church, chapel and community in Somercotes

Michael Dalling and Raymond Francis

The area

Located in East Lindsey, Lincolnshire, the village of 'Somercotes' comes under the Anglican Diocese of Lincoln which is coterminous with the old county of Lincolnshire. The East Lindsey District is the largest of Lincolnshire's local government districts both in area and population. Covering 175,000 hectares it extends from the centre of the county to the coast and from the boundary with Humberside to just north of Boston. The 1981 census records the population as 104,546 giving the area a population density of only 0.57 persons per hectare. Nevertheless, the area is experiencing a demographic increase. In common with the countrywide rate between 1981 and 1990 East Lindsey's population has increased from 105,000 to about 119,000.[1] This population increase, though small, contradicts the frequently voiced assumption that rural areas are experiencing further depopulation.

Somercotes lies on the east coast of East Lindsey some 10 miles (16 kilometres) north-east of the small market town of Louth and approximately 16 miles (26 kilometres) south of the large industrial conurbation of Grimsby. Comprising two spatially separate and quite different types of village, Somercotes is particularly suitable as a case-study of religion in rural areas. There are two divisions; one of these, North Somercotes, is substantially larger and because of its designation as a growth area it will continue to be so. The 1981 census records the population as 1,294, but we would estimate that this has increased by at least 100 today. White (1856, p. 236) recorded the population as 1953 in 1,841, rising to 1,039 in 1851; this appears to denote a relatively stable population. Nevertheless, demographic and industrial developments have brought noticeable social change. Though this area is predominantly agricultural, few are now employed in this capacity, and a majority commute to local towns. Moreover, demographic change has brought substantial 'new blood' into the village, but in no way could North Somercotes be regarded as a commuter area. The village still has a substantial indigenous population and a strong agricultural ethos. Many residents still have ties with the land and conversations in pubs and shops were found to be predominantly about crops, the weather, and other matters of relevance to agriculture.

By contrast South Somercotes is a small village two miles (3 kilometres) inland of its larger neighbour. If 'North' can be regarded as isolated, 'South' is even more so and can be said to be 'out in the sticks'. There is a central core to the village, but as a reflection of its agricultural origins many families live far removed from this. Those agricultural origins are equally pertinent today, and it can be said that the land forms the basis for 'South''s existence. Even the few newcomers have been attracted by the land attached to a property, or the 'good life' quality which the arcadian imagery of the village appears to offer.

Determination by inhabitants to preserve this timeless quality has led to a persistent refusal to allow further development. Success in this respect has ensured preservation, but at the price of stagnation. The village today no longer has a school, church or chapel. Only a shop and a pub remain, the latter having diversified into an Italian restaurant. Stagnation is also reflected in the declining population. The 1981 census records the population as 214, which is appreciably smaller than the 400 inhabitants noted by White (1856, p. 237).

Despite these differences, socially these two villages are to a large extent considered a single unit. Villagers refer to occurrences and locations as being at 'South' or 'North', but friendships and social gatherings are often a mixture without any sense of a person coming from another village. Nevertheless, 'North' and 'South' are very different, and separation and preservation of their distinct identities has historical precedent. During 1635, 120 acres (48.6 hectares) of marsh land were drained and allotted to the poor; 80

acres (32.4 hectares) were for the benefit of those at 'North' and 40 acres (16.2 hectares) for South Somercotes (*Kelly's Directory*, 1922, pp. 544-5; White, 1856, pp. 235-7). This charity for the benefit of the poor continues today; while changed in form, it maintains that separation. Most of the land has been sold, and benefits are taken from an investment account. Assessments are based on individual needs but generally recipients tend to be one-parent families or more commonly widows.[2]

Institutional religion

Historically, religion in Somercotes prior to the nineteenth century saw the Church of England unopposed. St Mary's Church, North Somercotes was founded by Robert Fitzgerald in 1184, but there must have been an earlier Saxon church. Fitzgerald appropriated the church to the Priory of Legbourne until the consecration of the Vicarage in 1213 by St Hugh (the famous Bishop of Lincoln), thereby ensuring a resident parish priest. The patronage later passed to the King (as Duke of Lancaster), who remains patron to this day of both North and South Somercotes churches. St Peter's, South Somercotes is unique in this area in that it is the only church to have a spire, which has led to its affectionate term 'Queen of the Marsh'. Of interest is the confusion that existed between the dedications of the two churches from 1681. The parish church of North Somercotes (St Mary's) was known as St Peter's, and that of South Somercotes (St Peter's) as St Mary's. This error was corrected 266 years later by the Diocesan Record Office after its discovery by the Rev. Reginald George Cowie, Vicar of North Somercotes from 1947 to 1952.

This traditional dominance of the Church of England was eroded during the nineteenth century by the spread of Methodism. Both the United Methodists and the Wesleyan Methodists built chapels in South Somercotes; while North Somercotes had Wesleyan, United Methodist and Primitive Methodist chapels as well as a Salvation Army Barracks (*Kelly's Directory*, 1922, pp. 544-5).

Ongoing rationalization has today seen the number of churches and chapels substantially reduced. The Primitive Methodist chapel was closed down in the 1960s, despite (according to informants) being well attended. These same informants revealed that at the time of the closure it was believed that the Primitive Methodists would attend the Wesleyan chapel, but few made the transition. At the time of the research reported here (mid-1987), South Somercotes still retained its chapel: but this has since closed. Both villages are now served by the chapel built on the site of the old Wesleyan chapel in 1836. Though a small building, it is well maintained and ideally suited to the congregation size, and it is centrally situated in the village. That Methodists see a viable future in Somercotes is evident by the extensive renovation work recently undertaken on the old manse. Moreover, it is clear that children are seen as an important link to that future. School visits, separate services designed specifically to be more enjoyable to children, and a strong emphasis on Sunday Schools all effectively ensure that the message of Methodism is spread at an early age. But it would be erroneous to equate these efforts of Methodists with a narrow, self-centred interest. Recent extensive and expensive reconstruction work by Methodists has provided the village with a youth centre.

Methodist practices can thus be seen as meeting not only spiritual, but also personal and social needs; and it is precisely in such respects that the Anglican church has shown its greatest neglect. Attempts from the 1850s by Anglican clergy to stem the rise of Methodism instigated a range of populist measures. But as Obelkevich (1976, pp. 103-82) has argued, as a method of social control these proved unsuccessful. It was not only a case of too little too late; but also did not address the need for a religion that was temporal as well as spiritual.

The Anglican incumbent during the period of research was on the Board of Governors of the Church of England Primary School. He sometimes sat in assemblies, but he was not prepared to speak at assembly or to take any classes. This refusal stemmed from his personal opposition to religion in schools unless it was broadly-based in content. There has not been an Anglican Sunday School for many years. The structural condition of the Anglican churches shows evidence of neglect. St Mary's church, in contrast to its Methodist counterpart, gives a clear impression of decay. The exterior shows evidence of ruin in places, despite the expenditure of substantial sums on makeshift repairs; and burial grounds are commonly overgrown and unkempt. Internally the situation is little better; one gets little impression of love and care, let alone glory. St Peter's showed signs of advanced decay before it was finally closed in 1988. It has subsequently been taken over by the Redundant Churches Fund. Some repairs are being carried out with a view to opening the building to the public because of its historic interest; but there are no plans to resume regular worship there.

Religion and the village

A misleading picture can be presented if one confines analysis of religion to its institutional aspects. Surveys of organized religion almost invariably show declining attendances and are usually accompanied by various explanations for this apparent trend to secularization in our modern society. Yet it was clear that a majority if not all villagers considered themselves to be Christian. There is also no doubt that these same people consider that they have the right to use the church on the odd occasion in life, regardless of whether or not they have made any contribution whatever to it.

These non-churchgoers as in the rest of the country constitute the majority, so on what do they base this right of membership? One criterion is obviously the fact that most of them will have been baptized. The debatable relevance of this is shown by Garbett (1960, p. 60), who states that out of every 100 children 67 are baptized, 34 attend Sunday School, 26 are confirmed and only 9 make their communion at Easter. One could not envisage a greater drop-out rate than this, which must question baptism as a basis for membership. These problems are exacerbated by the prescriptive nature of conventional definitions. It tends to be assumed that church supporters are to be equated with church attenders. However, it is evident in Somercotes that non-attenders at church considered themselves as church supporters through their attendance at such functions as fetes and bingo. This once again reiterates the dichotomy between church and religion, in that as far as villagers are concerned there is no necessary link between being a Christian, an active supporter of the church, and actually going to church.

That dichotomy is inevitable when the scope of religion is defined to the exclusion of folk religion, which many beliefs clearly are (Luckmann, 1967, p. 131; Towler, 1974, pp. 145-62; Obelkevich, 1976, p. 263). If one were to broaden the scope of 'religion' it would include not only these non-churchgoing people but also many other aspects of popular culture. This inclusion would no doubt disturb the true believer, yet we would argue that popular beliefs and practices are relevant for two reasons. Firstly, religion is prior to the church, both analytically and chronologically. In many cases Christianity superimposed its religious rites on pagan practices. Villagers have moulded certain institutional religious beliefs into what Obelkevich argues to be their 'personal *Weltanschauung*, a private theatre of sacred phenomena' (Obelkevich, 1976, p. 261).

82

Secondly, many previously sacred rites have lost all trace of religious content and, although they are still observed, this is a temporal rather than a spiritual activity.

That the wider village in its conception of folk religion embraces the church can be seen in the large attendances shown at church for the rites of passage. The majority of villagers may not be overtly religious, but there is a large attendance at burials. Death is now largely professionalized, and most of the traditional marks of respect are no longer observed: yet for many it is clear that religion via the church is the only way of making sense of this universal experience. The occasion is marked by sacredness, and few people go about their lives in a normal fashion after the death of a friend. Likewise at other rites of passage there is a similar high level of involvement from people who are normally religiously inactive. Weddings are occasions when the church building is often filled to capacity. It would be inaccurate to explain this phenomenon purely in terms of religious beliefs; rather it could be interpreted in terms of Gluckman's idea that ceremonies are a public demonstration of an individual's new social role (Gluckman, 1962). But when attending such occasions it becomes clear that a religious aura remains significant even for those who do not attend church regularly.

That few will take the vows of baptism seriously was acknowledged by the Anglican incumbent at the time of the research. Yet if he restricted these rites to active church or chapel members only, there is little doubt that the village would erupt in anger. These various aspects illustrate that while for many organized religion has little relevance to everyday life, religion *per se* is never absent. The meaning and relevance people give to various rites and rituals may be totally different from those of the church, but nevertheless their significance remains.

There are also some more central, structural aspects of organized religion that are relevant to folk religion. These can be seen in the ways that many of the church's holidays and rites have been reinterpreted. The Harvest Festival is one of the better attended church festivals, yet this celebration was unknown to the church until 1862. To an extent, occasions of this nature are a continuation of the pagan rites that used to be prevalent in this area. The following extract illustrating the meaning of corn dollies which are still a feature of Harvest Festivals illustrates this well:

Prayers be good enuff ez fur as they goas, but t'awmoighty mun
be strange an' throng wi' soa much corn to look after (Gutch and
Peacock, 1908, p. 209).

In reflecting the power of nature, the symbolism of the harvest
motif is also a reflection of the folk-religious influence (Clark, 1982,
pp. 104-6).

The case of Shrove Tuesday is a particularly good example of how
popular belief, while retaining the significance of the occasion, has
changed its meaning and the activities associated with it. In the
Christian calendar, Shrove Tuesday is for 'shriving' - confession
and absolution in preparation for Lent. But in Lincolnshire it
became 'fasten penny day', on which farm and domestic servants
were hired (Obelkevich, 1976, p. 266). It was also 'Pancake Tuesday',
from the traditional dish of the day. Far from being a time of
austerity, it was associated with feasting and leisure pursuits. It
becomes apparent from these few examples that religion is not to be
seen merely in terms of formal organizations. Rather religion has
a more universal applicability to village society than the narrow
confines of organizations or institutions. In many cases religious
beliefs and practices have become the subjects of myths,
superstitions and local customs, and as such form an integral part of
the local fabric. Such developments might be rejected by the
custodians of institutional religion, but this would not negate their
meaning or vitality. In view of the existence of such 'subterranean
theologies', Martin has maintained (for England as a whole) that
'far from being secular our culture wobbles between partially
absorbed Christianity ... and beliefs in fate, luck and moral
governance' (1967, p. 76). This certainly appears to be so, for while
many of these customs and practices were taken from accounts of
earlier times, they continue to have a legitimating influence upon
everyday life to the people of Somercotes. Whether in fact such
beliefs are compatible with institutional religion and its custodians
will be examined in the empirical study.

The study

After a successful pilot survey of the neighbouring village of
Theddlethorpe, a questionnaire survey in North and South
Somercotes was carried out. The intention of this survey was the
complete coverage of self-acknowledged church and chapel
members. For North Somercotes, Anglican respondents were

those on the Church Electoral Roll and the Methodists were those on the Full Membership Roll. For South Somercotes, both Anglican and Methodist attenders were very few in number, and the Anglican incumbent was reluctant to provide details of the few names on the Church Electoral Roll. Accordingly, it was decided for South Somercotes simply to note who were regular attenders at church and chapel, on both a visual and an investigative basis; and all of these were included in the survey. Thus for North Somercotes there were 51 Anglicans and 53 Methodists, and for South Somercotes 10 Anglicans and 7 Methodists. Notification of the research project was placed in the village magazine one month before the project commenced. Church and chapel ministers were also asked to make an announcement concerning the study, both to increase awareness and to encourage a positive response. Distribution of questionnaires was begun on 15 June 1987 and was completed on 4 July 1987. Total distribution amounted to 121 of which 89 were successfully completed giving a response rate of 73.6 per cent. In common with most surveys of religion, there were more women respondents (59 or 66.3 per cent) as opposed to men (30 or 33.7 per cent). There were also more Anglican than Methodist respondents (48 [53.9 per cent] as opposed to 41 [46.0 per cent]).

The number included in the study is therefore small; 121 questionnaires were distributed out of a total population of 1508 (1981 census); this represents 8.0 per cent of the population. This should be compared with the figure of 3.2 per cent for Anglicans on the Electoral Roll in England as a whole. For Methodist Full Members the figure for England is 0.9 per cent.[2] It appears that about 3-4 per cent of villagers attended church or chapel regularly, therefore (particularly for North Somercotes) it does not follow that those who were church or chapel 'members' were all regular attenders. As Garbett (1960, pp. 115-6) has suggested, there are generally three categories of membership: the active, the occasional and those who claim the benefits but rarely attend services. Somercotes people also follow national trends in relation to differing involvement by gender.

It is of interest to examine the relationship between the fraction of the community who are church or chapel members and the wider population of Somercotes. It has been argued earlier that the wider village community see themselves as active supporters through their attendance at church and chapel functions. However, replies to questionnaires only partly confirm this. In respect of weddings 72 respondents (80.9 per cent) affirmed the right of non-users to marry in church or chapel, while 78 (87.6 per cent) agreed that the children of non-users should be allowed to be christened. On the other hand, when asked if non-users who supported the church or chapel should be seen as active supporters, only 44 respondents (49.4 per cent) endorsed this point of view. This is surprising; the church and chapel rely substantially on the income generated by various functions, and without public support their financial viability would be in question. Many villagers in fact frequently expressed outrage at being constantly pestered for contributions while receiving nothing in return. But this does not appear to be acknowledged by respondents; only 23 (22.3 per cent) saw the parish as the ideal source for their income. The majority (38 or 36.9 per cent) believed personal giving should be the prime source with the remainder being fairly evenly divided between identifying the central church (22 or 21.4 per cent), the local authority (11 or 10.7 per cent), and the government (9 or 8.7 per cent) as the most appropriate source of funds.

The apparent confusion concerning the rights of non-users, and the evidence to which they could be considered as active supporters, was apparent in respondents' definition of a Christian. Table 4.1 shows the answers to the question 'How do you define a Christian?' according to the four choices presented on the questionnaire.

Table 4.1
Definition of a Christian

	N	%
Someone who goes to church regularly	20	22.5
Someone who is baptised	14	15.7
Someone who is confirmed	11	12.3
Something else	57	64.0

The majority, therefore, saw no necessary link between being a Christian and the church or chapel. There was space in which 'something else' could be indicated in more detail, and 38 such comments were received. A number, although mentioning Jesus or Christ, did so in what might be called a secular context, for example:

A person who believes in God and reacts to situations in a straightforward way, e.g. truthful, unselfish.

A second type of reply was totally religious in content:

Someone who believes in Jesus Christ as the Son of God.

There was also a third category that seemed to deny the involvement, institutional or otherwise, in their definition of a Christian:

Someone who cares, has loyalty, is helpful and can keep a confidence.

One who lives a near-Christian life, helps people, generally does good, but who does not have to attend church.

These replies illustrate the fact that respondents see little relationship between institutional religion and their definition of a Christian. Those showing the greatest degree of religious involvement chose Biblical definitions; but for a majority being a Christian is largely a matter of a humanitarian rather than a religious definition. This was substantially confirmed by the fact that 66 respondents (74.2 per cent) stated that they believed that a person who did 'good works' could be a Christian, even if he or she did not attend a place of worship.

Support for this proposition came from questions asking respondents about atheists and believers in non-Christian religions. On being asked where a person who does 'good works' but who does not attend a place of worship went on death, 63 (70.8 per cent) stated this to be 'Heaven'. In the case of believers in a non-Christian religion, 39 (43.8 per cent) indicated their destination as the Christian Heaven, with 16 (18.0 per cent) saying 'their Heaven'; 27 (30.3 per cent) said that they did not know the answer. In the case of atheists, 28 respondents (31.5 per cent) still thought that they would be admitted to Heaven, with only 6 (96.7 per cent) answering 'Hell'. Here the largest number answered 'Do not know' (50 or 56.2 per cent). It thus emerges that difficulties and uncertainties arise in respect of a person who *rejects* Christian belief, but that those who accept Christian belief but who do not attend church or chapel are still thought of as able to go to Heaven.

The overall pattern of these replies indicates that a majority of respondents do not see any necessary relationship between institutional involvement and definitions of a Christian, when related to the ultimate destination of an individual. Yet when they are presented with the problem of a person of non-Christian beliefs, or an atheist, their viewpoint changes. The fact that a person who does 'good works' may equally be an atheist or a Muslim does not seem to be considered. It appears that many see 'Heaven' as their exclusive club, but that membership of such a club does not necessarily involve active attendance at church or chapel.

A number of other questions produced replies which seemed to indicate the erosion of institutional influence. It was notable, for instance, that only 27 respondents (30.3 per cent) indicated a desire to be buried in the church or chapel graveyard. The reluctance of Anglicans towards having a church burial could possibly be attributed to the condition of the graveyard. Although recently improved, for many years this was in an unkempt condition exacerbated by the incumbent's practice of allowing goats access for grazing. Such conditions must act as a deterrent, but this would not explain the equal reluctance of Methodists, whose graveyard is well maintained. These answers must reflect a general move away from traditional patterns of behaviour concerning death; and this tendency was apparent in other responses. Thus only 13 respondents (14.6 per cent) said that they continued the practice of laying out the dead, while even fewer (11 or 12.4 per cent) continued to draw curtains or cover mirrors after a death in the family. When questioned all respondents remembered carrying out such practices in the past, but none could give reasons for having discontinued them.

It could be argued that the erosion of such traditional practices could be attributed to the fact that only 20 (22.5 per cent) were born in Somercotes. But this seems to be of little relevance since many had lived in Somercotes for a long time, and in any case such practices are not unique to the area. Moreover, many were born in surrounding villages. Even in respect of coffin bearers a majority of respondents (64 or 71.9 per cent) indicated a preference for this task to be carried out by professionals. This is a relatively stable rural society and certainly few people would lack family or friends to do this. In fact for many in the wider population one gets the impression that it is a matter of honour, almost a ritual, to carry their friends. Nevertheless, only 18 respondents (20.2 per cent) registered a wish to be carried by their family or friends; this seems to suggest that for a majority death is now treated in a functional and clinical manner, and has lost much of its religious significance. For respondents to choose not to be interred in the sanctified ground of their church or chapel must at least lead one to question the religious significance that they place on death. However, it must be remembered that cremation is generally approved by all churches. But there was no ambiguity when respondents were asked whether the lack of a Christian burial would have made much difference in the case of those such as soldiers who had died in battle without it. Only 12 respondents (13.5 per cent) felt it made a difference; for the majority (60 or 67.4 per cent), no religious significance was attached to the lack of a Christian burial in this respect. Moreover, even for the 12 respondents who said that it did make a difference, only 2 mentioned any religious significance, characteristically 'to make their peace with God'. For the remainder, it was a concern for bereaved relatives and friends that was the primary justification for a Christian burial. Typical replies of this nature were 'effect on the rest of the family' or 'for the family mostly'.

Erosion of traditional religious beliefs and practices was found in relation to other aspects of behaviour. The practice of 'churching' of women after giving birth to their children has now died out in this area; but 15 women (13 Anglicans and 2 Methodists) reported that they had been 'churched' in the past. In their attitudes to Shrove Tuesday, only 52 respondents (58.4 per cent) though of this day in terms of preparation for Lent. While this constitutes a majority, this cannot be seen as supportive of strong institutional belief from church and chapel members. This is so particularly since 20 respondents (22.5 per cent) attached no significance to the day, while for 13 (14.6 per cent) it signified nothing more than the annual pancake race. It would however be mistaken to see such findings as indicative of a lack of belief by respondents in their faith. Although Lent was apparently irrelevant to many, a religious interpretation of the main Christian festivals was strongly in evidence. Christmas was seen by 50 respondents (62.9 per cent) as primarily a religious occasion with only 27 (30.3 per cent) seeing the day in terms of a holiday or family occasion. Attitudes to Easter strongly emphasized the religious significance of the occasion: 77 respondents, or 86.5 per cent, saw it in this light, with only 5 (5.6 per cent) attaching no religious importance to this festival.

Christian faith was found to be particularly important in relation to respondents' children; 57 respondents (81.4 per cent of those who had children) maintained that their children were attending Sunday School or had done so in the past. Furthermore, not only did 82 respondents (92.1 per cent) consider that religion should be taught at school, but a majority (67 or 75.3 per cent) were of the opinion that children should be taught that Christianity is the one and true faith. 81 (91.0 per cent) said that religious instruction should take place in both primary and secondary schools. When asked whether such teaching should be centred on Christianity or whether it should consist of comparative religion, 47 respondents (52.8 per cent) preferred teaching to be mainly about Christianity, while only 34 (38.2 per cent) preferred the teaching of religion to be comparative. Comparative religion is taught at the secondary school, and apparently a majority of respondents do not agree with this policy. Of interest also is the disparity between the earlier question where 67 respondents (75.3 per cent) stated that children should be taught that Christianity is the true faith, and the 34 (38.2 per cent) indicating a preference for comparative religion. This indicates that while a number of respondents believe that comparative religion should be taught, many also consider that other religions should be placed in a subordinate position to Christianity.

Anglican-Methodist differences

Respondents registered broad agreement on many issues, but throughout the survey certain differences were often apparent between church and chapel members. Such a difference was evident in relation to confirmation and full membership figures. 45 Anglicans (93.8 per cent) said that they had been confirmed, but only 26 Methodists (63.4 per cent) stated that they were full members. Possible explanation for this difference is that children in this area are taught in the Church of England primary school, leading to an acceptance of Church of England values and probably to confirmation at an early age. In contrast many Methodists were found to have made their commitment later in life, when it would be more difficult to undergo a personal ritual in public. A difference was also apparent in relation to respondents' children; 28 offspring of Anglicans (58.3 per cent) had been confirmed, in contrast to only 10 (24.4 per cent) of the offspring of Methodists who had become full members. It was also apparent that Methodists attached greater religious significance to the attainment of full membership by their children than did Anglicans in respect of confirmation. Typical replies given by Anglicans were:

So that they were full members if they wanted to be, and wouldn't need to be confirmed as adults.

To give them a fuller background to life, e.g. there is more to life than money.

By contrast typical Methodist replies were:

To commit their lives into God's service, and promise to follow in his steps.

Belonging to the family of God.

The primary determinant of denominational allegiance was found to be parents, with 66 respondents (74.2 per cent) following in their parents' footsteps. Only 18 respondents differed from this; and of the 17 who gave reasons for the change, none gave a doctrinal reason. For 2 women it was marriage; another wished to join the choir, while a fourth stated that his parents were not Christian. The majority of respondents (13) who had changed their allegiance said that it had been because of dissatisfaction with the church. A typical reply was:

I felt I did not belong to the church any more, and found fellowship and friendship in the Methodist church.

Replies of this nature positively reinforce the idea that institutional worship is as much a social as a religious activity. It is noteworthy that no Methodist had changed religious allegiance.

The replies to various questions threw some light on the extent to which church or chapel activity was to be seen in primarily religious or in social terms. The relevance of religion to everyday life can be seen as related to the strength of personal belief; and questions relating to private devotion received a high positive response. In some cases there was no major difference between Anglicans and Methodists. That the overwhelming majority of all respondents found their faith supportive is evident in the fact that 79 (88.8 per cent) declared that they regularly prayed privately. Furthermore, 78 (88.8 per cent) believed that those prayers were answered, while 79 (88.8 per cent) stated that they derived strength from their faith. Such private religiosity was seen to be complemented by church or chapel attendance, with 55 respondents (61.8 per cent) affirming that they attended at least on a weekly basis, and 18 (20.2 per cent) on a regular basis. On this there was a certain tendency to exaggerate; church and chapel records did not confirm such a level of attendance.

But despite this level of activity claimed, there was some conflict with orthodox religious beliefs since respondents by no means infrequently chose secular options. For example, Table 4.2 shows that only 53 respondents (59.6 per cent) indicated a belief in God. It was to be expected that theism would be generally subscribed to among a population of self-professed religious persons. An identical level of belief is found in the case of the Resurrection, and again this would seem to be a central tenet for Christians.

Table 4.2
Religious beliefs

	Affirmative responses	
	N	%
God	53	59.6
Virgin Birth	43	48.3
Devil	26	29.2
Resurrection	53	59.6
Reincarnation	15	16.9
Evolution	23	25.8

Question: 'Would you tick which of these you believe in? (followed by the list above).

This suggests that the rural church does not constitute a fundamentalist remnant such as is often found in urban areas. It is also of interest that 36 (40.4 per cent) of respondents overall saw God as something to give depth to life, rather than as a supreme being (an option favoured by 56 [62.9 per cent]); some gave more than one choice.

In most cases there were no major differences between Methodists and Anglicans. However, this was not so in respect of beliefs concerning the Virgin Birth. Table 4.3 shows that Methodist women in particular have an especially low level of belief in this. Discussions with the Methodist minister to see if there were theological differences between the two groups to account for the variation showed that there was not. However, he did state that the doctrine was not emphasized by the Methodists to the extent that it was in the Church of England.

Table 4.3
Belief in the Virgin Birth

| | Anglican | | | | Methodist | | | |
| | Men | | Women | | Men | | Women | |
	N	%	N	%	N	%	N	%
Believe	11	61.1	20	66.6	5	41.7	7	24.1
No not believe	7	38.9	10	33.3	7	58.3	22	75.9
	11	100.0	30	99.9	12	100.0	29	100.0

Table 4.4
Creation of man by God or evolution

	N	%
God	56	62.9
Evolution	10	11.2
Both	22	24.7
No answer	1	1.1
	89	99.9

Question: Do you believe man was created by God or by evolution? (3 choices, as above).

Table 4.4 presents respondents' views on whether man was created by God or evolution; it shows that a majority have a traditional view. It is of interest that only 22 respondents chose 'Both' as the answer, as this is the belief favoured by both ministers. It would appear that congregations are either rejecting ministers' opinions, or alternatively that those ministers are not preaching sufficiently on this subject. Table 4.5 once again shows a large difference between female Anglicans and female Methodists.

Methodists can be seen to have more traditional views on this subject than do Anglicans. But despite this disparity, it can be seen that both groups clearly tend towards traditional views on the subject, although this does not necessarily indicate total disbelief in evolution or belief in creationism.

Table 4.5
God and Evolution: Anglican-Methodist differences (females)

	Anglicans		Methodists	
	N	%	N	%
God	17	56.7	23	79.3
Evolution	2	6.7	2	6.9
Both	11	36.7	4	13.8
	30	100.1	29	100.0

Anglican-Methodist differences were particularly noteworthy in questions relating to ministers. As can be seen from Table 4.6, a larger proportion of Methodists (73.2 per cent) consider that ministers have a demanding life than do Anglicans. This may be partly due to local differences; the Anglican vicar had at the time of the research only two churches under his care, whereas the Methodist minister was responsible for seven and was soon to acquire an eighth.

Table 4.6
Whether ministers have a life of ease

	Anglicans		Methodists	
	N	%	N	%
Yes	19	39.6	5	12.2
No	25	52.1	30	73.2
No answer	4	8.3	6	14.6
	48	100.0	41	100.0

Question: Do you think that ministers, on the whole, have a life of ease?

This is not to infer that the Methodist minister automatically has to work harder; he has a large organized body of helpers, but the number of chapels under his care can influence opinions. However, the difference between the two groups could also be because of differences between the expectations of church and

94

chapel members concerning the minister's role. There was no marked difference between Methodists and Anglicans concerning attitudes to the *principle* of ministers visiting; 84 respondents (94.4 per cent) answered that they should do so, one of the strongest responses in the survey. However, only 36 respondents (40.4 per cent) considered the present level of visiting to be satisfactory. There was, however, a major difference between the Anglicans and the Methodists on this issue, as Table 4.7 shows:

Table 4.7
Level of satisfaction with frequency of pastoral visitation[3]

| | Anglicans | | Methodists | |
	N	%	N	%
Yes, satisfied	6	12.5	30	73.2
No, not satisfied	35	72.9	7	17.1
No answer	7	14.6	4	9.8
	48	100.0	41	100.1

Methodists seemed largely satisfied with their minister's level of visiting, although he had seven parishes to cover. It was thought possible that the Methodist respondents had made allowance for this, but further talks with a number of respondents revealed that this was not the case. Additionally, during an interview with the Methodist minister he expressed regret that the size and widespread area to which he had to minister made personal contact difficult: but even so, he appears to be largely meeting his congregation's wishes.

The size of the negative Anglican vote is extraordinary, and initially suggests that the vicar is not meeting the wishes of his congregation for visitation. Older respondents tended to speak with fondness of a vicar who was the incumbent some years ago. They state that he was a 'man of the people', and express the wish for such a man now. The idea of a 'man of the people' rather than a 'man of the church' supports earlier suggestions concerning the social significance of the church to its members. When the matter of visiting was raised with the Anglican incumbent, he maintained that it was a myth that parishioners wished him to call on them. He argued that during his first year in Somercotes he made a determined effort to carry out this practice, but found it a pointless exercise. Apart from the fact that many people are away at work during the day, his experience was that the majority were embarrassed by his presence. He tells of one house where, when he knocked on the door, the husband called out 'The fire's gone out and the vicar's at the door'. The only question this left him was not whether he was unwelcome but which was the greater evil. He maintains that he is quite willing to visit anyone who expresses a wish for this, but he argues that few do. On balance his argument seems persuasive, giving the impression that while parishioners like the idea of the vicar visiting, it is to other people and not to themselves. Nevertheless, this leaves unexplained the difference between Anglican and Methodist responses to this question.

That respondents see a minister's role in social terms was evident in a number of questions. On being asked whether ministers can help with personal problems, 77 (86.5 per cent) believed this to be so. Moreover, 39 respondents (43.8 per cent) stated that they had received help in this respect from ministers in the past. But again there was a marked difference between Anglicans and Methodists, as Table 4.8 shows.

Table 4.8
Respondents who had received help from ministers[4]

	Anglicans		Methodists	
	N	%	N	%
Yes, had received	16	33.3	23	56.0
No, had not received	31	64.6	16	39.0
No answer	1	2.1	2	4.9
	48	100.0	41	99.9

Confirming earlier findings, Table 4.8 shows that Methodist ministers perform more of a social role than do Anglican vicars. However, all respondents seem to place particular emphasis upon the pastoral role when indicating what they see as desired qualities of ministers of religion. This is suggested in Table 4.9:[5]

Table 4.9
Desired qualities of a minister

	N	%
Man of great human understanding	74	83.1
Outstanding preacher	0	0
Brilliant organizer	1	1.1
Man of great sanctity	8	9.0
No answer	6	6.7
	89	99.9

The centrality of a minister's social role assumes a new focus when compared with the importance of church buildings to respondents. When asked 'Do you consider that the church/chapel building is more important than the vicar/minister?, notable differences were again found between Methodists and Anglicans.

Table 4.10
Whether building more important than minister

	Anglicans		Methodists	
	N	%	N	%
Yes	25	52.1	5	12.2
No	18	37.5	29	70.7
No answer	5	10.4	7	17.1
	48	100.0	41	100.0

Table 4.10 shows a complete contrast between the two groups. For Anglicans the building is more important, but for Methodists it is the minister. This appears to confirm a remark made by the Anglican vicar that 'Anglicans worship the bricks and mortar rather than the religious message'. Nevertheless, an additional factor is that Anglicans have shown dissatisfaction with their vicar, and that perhaps many feel there is no religious message to be had from him. As such they quite possibly feel that vicars come and go

(whether they are perceived to be doing a useful job or not), whereas the church remains as a visible focus of their religious feelings.

For Methodists the reverse is the case; for them the building is shown to have relatively little importance. In itself this may seem surprising in view of the time, energy and money that Methodists have expended on the renovation of chapel buildings. But the importance of ministers to Methodists has been shown throughout, especially when it comes to meeting the needs of parishioners. Therefore the religious message focuses upon the minister, rather than the building. To an extent these findings again indicate the greater *Gemeinschaft* of Methodists, in that they are more interested in fellowship than in religious buildings. Confirmation of this is seen in Table 4.11, which shows that Methodists are far more willing to use house-groups than their Anglican counterparts.

Table 4.11
Attitudes to house-groups

	Anglicans		Methodists	
	N	%	N	%
Positive	19	39.6	22	53.6
Negative	25	52.1	17	41.5
No answer	4	8.3	2	4.9
	48	100.0	41	100.0

Question: If there was no church/chapel in the village and you were unable to travel would you consider house-groups as an alternative?

Whilst such findings provide further confirmation of the greater *Gemeinschaft* orientation of Methodists, it was clear that the church or chapel as a source of friendship was important to all respondents. When asked if they considered themselves as part of a family of worshippers, 68 (76.4 per cent) of all respondents stated that this was so. Moreover, while most respondents gained the majority of their friendships from the wider village, friendships developed through the church or chapel came a close second. Such findings indicate that religion in this area exercises a more pervasive influence for many respondents than purely weekly attendance. It is also strongly indicative of the fact that church or chapel involvement is at least as much a social as a religious activity. Yet some found the social ingredient missing: and this was particularly true of Anglicans. Moreover, respondents looked for social leadership from ministers of religion, and in this the Anglican incumbent was perceived to be neglectful.

This survey shows that the majority of respondents see the role of the vicar as temporal rather than spiritual. Emphasis was placed on the pastoral duties of understanding and visiting, rather than the spiritual aspects such as 'holiness' or spreading of the Gospel. Somercotes is far from unique in this respect; other studies show that pastoral visitation was seen as particularly important by parishioners (ABC Television, 1964, p. 10).

The historical context is of interest here. During the mid-1800s visiting was seen as essential by both parishioners and bishops, although for different reasons. For parishioners it was for the promotion of temporal welfare, but for bishops it was seen as a way of combating Methodism. None the less, dissatisfaction with the level of Anglican visiting seems not to be a recent development. Obelkevich (1976, p. 166) points out that the regular exhortations from bishops on the subject made it clear that many clergy were negligent in this duty. In a more contemporary vein, Garbett (1960, p. 95) has drawn attention to the decline in the great tradition of pastoral visitation in the Anglican church. There are various possible explanations for the difference between Anglicans and Methodists in respect of pastoral visitation, but differences in recruitment levels must be a factor. The number of Methodist ministers has in the recent past been stated to be satisfactory (see Pickering, 1961, pp. 18-19), whereas during the period 1901-61 Anglican clergy declined in number by 20 per cent (Wilson, 1966, p. 78). Differences in the number of lay leaders and in the uses to which they are put also work to the disadvantage of the Anglicans. The problem of insufficient clergy was a primary reason for the Anglican church to revive in 1866 the ancient office of lay-reader, but despite substantial numbers their use is often limited and restricted. Somercotes has two licenced lay-readers, but neither of them practises because of differences with the present incumbent. Moreover, although for the Anglicans there are 7203 licenced readers in England as a whole, these are insignificant in comparison with the 13,170 Methodist local preachers[6] (bearing in mind that the Anglican church is larger). Within Somercotes Methodist local preachers perform a valuable role in taking services, in stewardship and in Bible classes and Sunday Schools: in fact in all aspects of the church. This closer involvement and greater integration by Methodists in their church is a further example of their *Gemeinschaft* orientation.

These differences are compounded by training and selection procedures. For Anglicans the General Ministerial Examination which is intended to assess candidates for the ordained and professional lay ministries now comprises six main subjects. 'Pastoral Studies' is now part of the syllabus, but only as an introductory course. There is also evidence of inadequacy in the time spent in pastoral placements: though it is understood that there have been changes in response to criticisms of this nature. If there is insufficient training for pastoral activities, this is unfair to both the parish and the incumbent. His 'calling' and grounding in religion may be beyond fault, but there will inevitably be problems if he has received little or no training which would enable him to operate on a social level. Yet as the survey showed, respondents indicated overwhelmingly that the most desired quality of a minister was 'a man of great human understanding'. This, coupled with the expressed wish for a 'man of the people', and a greater level of visitation, shows respondents' wish for a more temporal, pastoral care rather than spiritual; and Anglican ministers' training is not geared to meet this.

In contrast Methodist ministers go through a long treadmill in various lay capacities, being constantly assessed. There is of course no assumption that most lay preachers will have a calling for the ordained ministry. But it is a requirement that anyone wishing to be a minister should first be a lay preacher for at least two or three years. Even after this period of preparation, some would-be ministers fail selection: their ability to preach might not be in dispute, but many additional abilities are looked for in a candidate for ordination. The end product is a minister more attuned to his parishioners and more able to cope with whatever demands his ministry may make upon him.

That these problems are becoming recognized by the Anglican establishment is evident from the report of the Archbishops' Commission on Rural Areas, 1989-90 (Faith in the Countryside, 1990). In this report, it is recognized by the Board of Ministry that specific training is required by rural ministries, and it is recommended that a more developed training for curates likely to take rural incumbencies should be provided (Welsh, 1990, p. 64). Moreover, there is open recognition that many vicars are not worth much and that they require weeding out (Williamson, 1990, p. 58).

Yet despite that recognition, structural problems severely inhibit change. Out of 238 incumbents in the Lincoln Diocese, 87 are 55 or more years old and currently there are 36 vacancies (Williamson, 1990, p. 58-60). The shortfall is made worse by an economic crisis related to the low church attendance in this area.

For parishioners, such problems assume a more personal meaning. The continued closure of churches has been accompanied by an increase in the number of parishes under an incumbent's care. For example, in Somercotes St Peter's has closed, but a further two parishes have been assigned to the incumbent. Consequently his ability to take part in social activities, and to carry out the wishes of his parishioners for a greater level of visitation has been severely limited. Similarly, the economic problems of the church have seen a sustained campaign to coerce parishioners to increase their level of giving. This has in the main taken the form of appeals for covenants to be made of ten per cent of annual income. This economic coercion has annoyed both church- and non-churchfolk, and many have seen it as moral blackmail. In turn the yearly quotas have increased annually. At the last Annual General Meeting of the Anglican Parochial Church Council (PCC), parishioners were informed by the incumbent that quotas were going to increase by fifty per cent over the next three years.

Continued closure of churches is perhaps inevitable in view of the national decline in congregation numbers. There is now evidence of a decline not only in church attendance, but also in use of the church for rites of passage. As regards Methodism, Pickering (1961, pp. 27-8) quotes the Commission of Rural Methodism which argues that the poverty of worship will destroy Methodism. While such findings in respect of Methodists were not confirmed by the present study, the different focus of the two approaches is of great interest. For Anglicans the concern is with declining numbers, whereas for Methodists the concern is with a decline in faith. Nevertheless, these factors have helped to push both churches and chapels along the path of economic rationalization, and in doing so they have adopted attitudes similar to those of industry. Churches which have been ticking along for centuries are now being closed as uneconomic at a greatly increased rate. In consequence, as Wilson argues (1966, p. 139), religious functionaries who were once concerned with the service of God have increasingly come to serve the organization.

The establishment of a rational bureaucracy inevitably leads to unity as the most logical solution to the problem of empty pews. The specific ideals which caused denominations to come into being, namely differences in religious beliefs and practices, are seen as peripheral from the standpoint of the financial corporate mentality. The fact that church leaders are prepared to sacrifice these ideals to the more rational use of resources shows on the one hand their acceptance of the weakening of the religious ethic and on the other a wish to protect their profession.

In this area the dominant clerical cause in recent years has been the drive towards ecumenism. The nearby parish of Saltfleetby recently celebrated fifteen years of unity and on 10 June 1987, the Anglican and Methodist churches of Somercotes committed themselves to work and worship together more closely in a Local Ecumenical Project. The attraction of ecumenism to priests is plain; as Wilson argues (1966, p. 129), the loss of possible influence is preferable to the disappearance of large numbers of appointments. Equally, for the majority - the 'unchurched' - it must mean little difference apart from possibly fewer people knocking on the door for donations. But for the small core of regular worshippers it must mean a major upheaval, and this may be experienced differently by Anglicans and Methodists. As the survey has shown, there are major differences between them as to what constitutes the church. For Anglicans it is very much the building, whereas for Methodists it is not only the chapel, school room and youth club, but the whole Methodist community.

The impression one gets from clergy, both locally and nationally (see Turner-Smith, 1986) is that while they are quite willing to go along with these developments, ecumenical projects are in fact the will of the people. However, to assume that unity is the logical outcome of religious thought is to neglect the fact that organized religion cannot be interpreted without reference to the rest of society. People attend church or chapel for a variety of reasons other than religious, as this study has confirmed. Moreover, there is evidence of marked differences between Anglican and Methodist beliefs and practices, and unity was quite clearly not wanted by parishioners. Respondents not only freely voiced their objections, but it was sometimes apparent during attendance at joint services that parishioners were voting with their feet and not attending. Similar behaviour from respondents was observed over the closure of St Peter's; debates over this issue brought to the fore some of the strange idiosyncracies of PCCs. At the time when the issue of closure was broached no objections were given, and the PCC in fact voted for the closure. Yet during conversations with PCC members it was evident that there was clearly a strong undercurrent of opinion against this measure, which was confirmed by their reluctance to attend St Mary's. The vicar, who clearly supported the closure, wanted the congregation to attend St Mary's and was clearly exasperated by their refusal to do so.

The survey showed that only 55 per cent of respondents would attend an alternative place of worship if their own closed, which is hardly sufficient to justify an ecumenical movement. The difficulties surrounding proposals for amalgamation have been shown in other studies. An earlier survey of lay members of Anglican and Methodist churches in four towns (Clark, 1965) showed major differences in relation to communion, liturgy, hymn singing and sermons. These differences are all too clearly apparent in Somercotes, and particularly in relation to communion. Many Anglicans not only considered it wrong for Methodists to take communion, but also did not consider Methodist ministers to be qualified to give it. These difficulties are seen to arise from two factors. In the first place, Anglicans need to be confirmed before they may take communion, and consequently they consider it wrong that Methodists are allowed to take it without being confirmed. Secondly, problems arise from the interpretation and meaning given to the apostolic succession. Historically, careful provision for the preservation of continuity of the apostolic succession was made by the consecration of Archbishop Parker (Garbett, 1960, p. 15). Methodists chose to disregard this continuity by authorizing laymen to administer the sacrament, and in fact as Wilson points out (1966, p. 156), it was not until 1932, after the final union, that the laying on of hands became a feature of the Methodist church. These are not only fundamental historical and religious differences, but they lie at the heart of many people's faith and should not be disregarded.

Another problem is largely temporal, and this involves the organizational differences between the two. Even if basic understandings can be reached, ecumenism threatens the autonomy of the small core who are accustomed to running the affairs of their church or chapel. There is bound to be the fear of possible loss of individual status, together with the fear of 'their' church being swallowed by the more successful unit. These are real problems which cannot be sidetracked or neglected. Moreover, they cannot be seen as a logical response to increasing secularization and declining congregations. Ecumenism neglects not only the 'vast sea of unchurched' (Pickering, 1961, p. 31); it also neglects fundamental theological and social differences. The neglect of those differences by the 'church' is further demonstration of the dichotomy between respondents' religious beliefs and institutional beliefs and practices.

Conclusion

The religiously active in Somercotes constitute a minority, if the criterion to be taken is that of involvement in patterns of institutional worship. This can easily lead one to assume that the relevance of religion is minimal, with practitioners consisting of a predominantly aged, middle-class group constituting little more than a dying bourgeois cult. But this would be erroneous; a high level of religiosity is apparent both among churchgoers and the rest, if different criteria are seen as important. Much depends, however, on what is seen as coming within the scope of 'religion'. In many cases it seems that Somercotes people have evolved their own religious beliefs and have developed their own criteria concerning the definition of a 'Christian'.

Major differences were found between Anglicans and Methodists in respect of theological orientation. Moreover, Methodists not only had a clearer understanding of religious doctrine, but such doctrine also had a greater relevance to their daily lives. Of interest in this respect is a comment by the Anglican vicar:

> For me your most interesting conclusion is that there is a firmer grasp of Christian truths among Methodists than among Anglicans. I would have thought this would be so, but it is nice to have it demonstrated.

However, the theological differences that have been identified are minor in comparison with the relative satisfaction of their needs from religious activity. For all respondents, going to church was as much a social as a religious activity. The failure of the Anglican church to meet this need had led to some members changing allegiance, and to a majority registering dissatisfaction, particularly in relation to the level of visitation. By contrast the Methodist church met this social need for its members, and its spirit of *Gemeinschaft* was found to extend outwards into the wider religious community.

The Anglican church does not appear to be concerned over the smallness of its congregations, except in so far as this relates to financial contributions. The Weberian scenario of bureaucratic rationality that now appears to dominate the Anglican church has

104

made the saving of souls secondary to economic viability. The situation is a national one, tersely expressed by the Anglican vicar: 'Too few ministers, too many God-boxes, too many nominal Christians'. Incumbents attempting to work within such conflicting parameters face an impossible task, that of the raising of ever-increasing finances from an ever-diminishing source.

Both church and chapel appear to be attempting to solve their problems by unification; however, there are sufficient signs to indicate that rather than solving them, unification will tend to exacerbate such problems. Respondents indicated a high level of personal religiosity in terms of private prayer and the meaning and strength derived from prayer. However, the most striking result to come from the survey was the high degree of social satisfaction, of love and friendship, that respondents needed to get from organized religion. In a narrow sense this shows a secular attitude, in that religion becomes subordinate to the social. Nevertheless, if we accept the argument that religion exists to meet certain social needs, then the social aspect can be seen as an acceptable part of religion.

Respondents have shown that this is what they expect from religion: much more than a sterile one hour a week message. Methodism has shown itself to be largely capable of meeting those expectations, but whether Anglicanism can do this is problematic. Historically Anglicanism has not been able to meet this demand, and to do so today would involve a major transformation. In particular, training procedures are seen to be inadequate to equip incumbents for the social role demanded by parishioners. Moreover the Anglican church is hindered by the low priority that it appears to give to the active involvement of lay members. By contrast, Methodism in its extensive use of lay members has lightened the minister's work load and created an ethos of *Gemeinschaft*. That ethos has been shown to extend into the community, outside the immediate ambit of religious activity. Such community involvement is what is expected of religion by both outsiders and insiders.

Notes

1. Information from East Lindsey District Council, personal communication.

2. The Anglican figure is taken from Church of England (1988), p. 167). The Methodist figure is from Methodist Conference (1987), p. 45.

3. The two relevant questions were 'Do you think vicars/ministers should go round visiting people?' and 'Do you consider that yours does this sufficiently?'

4. The two relevant questions were 'Do you think vicars/ministers can be helpful in dealing with personal problems?' and 'Have you been helped in this way?'

5. The question was 'Could you tick just one of these qualities as being most desired of a minister?'. The question was based on Thompson (1957), p. 100 (see also pp. 33-4, 48-9, 61-2, 76).

6. The Anglican figure is taken from Church of England, Central Board of Finance (1987), p. 21. The Methodist figure is from Methodist Conference (1987), p. 49.

References

ABC Television (1965), *Television and Religion*, ABC Television, London.

Argyle, M. (1961), *Religious Behaviour*, Routledge and Kegan Paul, London.

Brothers, J. (1971), *Religious Institutions*, Longman, London.

Church of England (1988), *Church of England Year Book, 1988*, Church House, London.

Church of England, Central Board of Finance (1987), *Church Statistics: Facts and Figures about the Church of England*, Church House, London.

Clark, D. (1982), *Between Pulpit and Pew: Folk Religion in a North Yorkshire Fishing Village (Staithes)*, Cambridge University Press, Cambridge.

Clark, D.B. (1965), *Survey of Anglicans and Methodists in Four Towns*, Epworth Press/Church Information Office, London.

Diocese of Lincoln (1990), *The Challenge of Change in the Countryside*, Submission to the Archbishops' Commission on Rural Areas, Gemini Printers, Boston.

Faith in the Countryside: a Report presented to the Archbishops of Canterbury and York (1990), Churchman Publishing, Worthing.

Garbett, C. (1960), *The Claims of the Church of England* (abridged edition), Hodder and Stoughton, London.

Gluckman, M. (1962), 'Les Rites de Passage', in Gluckman (ed.), *Essays on the Ritual of Social Relations*, Manchester University Press, Manchester, pp. 1-52.

Gutch, E. and Peacock, M. (1908), *Examples of Printed Folklore concerning Lincolnshire*, Nutt, London.

Kelly's Directories Ltd. (1922), *Kelly's Directory of Lincolnshire with the City of Hull*, 10th ed., Kelly's Directories Ltd., London.

Luckmann, T. (1967), *The Invisible Religion*, Macmillan, London.

Martin, D. (1967), *A Sociology of English Religion*, SCM Press, London.

Methodist Conference (1987), *Minutes and Yearbook of the Methodist Conference*, Methodist Conference Office, London.

Obelkevich, J. (1976), *Religion and Rural Society: South Lindsey 1875-1925*, Clarendon Press, Oxford.

Pickering, W.S.F. (1961), *Anglican-Methodist Relations: Some Institutional Factors*, Longman and Todd, London.

Thompson, R.H.T. (1957), *The Church's Understanding of Itself*, SCM, London.

Towler, R. (1974), *Homo Religiosus: Sociological Problems in the Study of Religion*, Constable, London.

Turner-Smith, J.M. (1986), *Views from the Pews* (1986), British Council of Churches/ Catholic Truth Society, London.

Welsh, P. (1990), 'Training for Rural Ministry', in Diocese of Lincoln, p. 64.

White, W. (1856), *History, Gazetteer and Directory of Lincolnshire, and the City and Diocese of Lincoln*, William White, Sheffield.

Williamson, D. (1990), 'How the Diocese Works', in Diocese of Lincoln, pp. 57-63.

Wilson, B. (1966), *Religion in Secular Society*, Watts, London.

Wright, D. (1965), *Attitudes towards the Church in Wellingborough*, University of Leicester, Leicester (Vaughan College Papers No. 9).

Unpublished source

Woolfe, M. (Vicar of North Somercotes, 1958-73) (1975), Manuscripts concerning the history of St Mary's.

5 Churches and war: Attitudes during the Gulf conflict

Martin Shaw and Roy Carr-Hill

War poses the most difficult of challenges to Christians. Throughout history, wars have been times of tension between fundamental religious beliefs and the demands of secular power. Christian theology has sought to reconcile these issues with the doctrine of the 'just war', but this doctrine has become particularly difficult to apply in modern times. Weapons of mass destruction have tended to make twentieth-century war inherently genocidal, invalidating some of the conditions for the acceptability of war to Christian morality. At the same, mass - especially democratic - politics has tended to give war new dimensions of legitimacy, which it has been difficult for Christians to gainsay.

However the theological problems may be defined, church leaders and members have to grapple with these issues as questions as practical moral questions. The conflict which broke out in August 1990, as a result of Iraq's invasion of Kuwait, posed them in particularly acute forms. Iraq's actions were flagrant violations of international law, as well as cruel disruptions of the lives of all who lived in Kuwait. Few in the Western world disagreed with the decisions of their leaders, with United Nations backing, to impose sanctions and send military forces, to protect Saudi Arabia from a possible threat of Iraqi invasion and to put pressure on Iraq to withdraw from Kuwait. More difficult, however, was the issue of whether it was justified to wage war to force Iraq's retreat; and yet this issue was quickly posed, as American-led forces built up far beyond defensive levels, and the UN set deadlines for Iraqi withdrawal beyond which war would almost certainly be undertaken.

Christian leaders responded in varying ways to these developments. It is beyond the scope of this chapter to discuss the range of positions which were adopted, although we intend to examine this question in further research (Shaw, 1995 [forthcoming]). Given that our concern is with English attitudes, it is particularly relevant to note that no major national religious figure came out in a fundamental criticism of the war against Iraq, in which the British government and forces participated. The retiring Archbishop of Canterbury, Dr Robert Runcie, who was the only British Christian leader widely reported in the mass media, gave the government's policy his support, although he also expressed some anguish over the issue. On the other hand, Pope John Paul II, spiritual leader of the Catholic community, was an outspoken critic of the Western governments' position. Clearly this was an issue on which authoritative Christian opinion was divided.

The research

Our concern in this chapter, however, is not with leaders: the question we seek to answer is how did Christians at grass roots level respond to the challenge of the Gulf War? The research reported here is part of a programme of survey research into people's attitudes, carried out during and immediately after the war. We formulated two postal questionnaires, the first of which was sent out and replied to in February 1991, during the second half of the war, and the second of which was sent out and replied to during late March and early April 1991, within a few weeks of the end of the war.

The first questionnaire was sent out to a random sample of 1300 drawn from the electoral register in the four consituencies of Hull and Beverley, but also to complete populations of certain specialist groups in North Humberside, including all ministers of religion (of all denominations) listed in the Hull area telephone directory. The second questionnaire was distributed to a similar-sized random sample of the same general population, including approximately 500 of those who had responded to the first questionnaire. This survey was not extended to any specialist groups. Responses to the random sample surveys were just over 40 per cent, for the first questionnaire, and slightly under this figure for the second (good response rates for postal questionnaires in these circumstances). The response from the group of clergy was just under 30 per cent.

The methodology and general findings of the surveys have been described in a research report issued at the end of March 1991, and in subsequent articles (Shaw and Carr-Hill, 1991a, 1991b, 1992; see also Shaw, 1991). While we cannot claim that a sample drawn from the population of North Humberside is statistically representative of anything more than that population, we know of no specific reasons why our findings should not be broadly applicable to the general population of England. Our sample, with 80 per cent approval of British involvement in the war, closely mirrored the national picture portrayed in numerous opinion polls.

The main differences between our sample and the known characteristics of the national population can be summarised as a slight over-representation of the manual working class, council tenants and Labour voters (although this is compensated for in our results by a slight under-representation of these groups among respondents); and, more seriously, a strong under-representation of ethnic and religious minorities (Muslims, who responded very distinctively to the Gulf War, were virtually absent from our samples).

A less measurable distinctiveness of the Hull area is the historic experience of war in the city, which gained an anonymous notoriety in the Second World War among as the 'North-east coast town' most regularly bombed by the Germans among all large British towns except London. This may have affected the responses of some older people to the war.[1] Another local dimension, which may account (for example) for the relatively high level of concern expressed for family and friends involved in the Gulf, is the relatively high level of military recruitment, reflecting Hull's low-wage, less-skilled and high-unemployment economy. The local paper, the *Hull Daily Mail*, reflected this with a constant flow of 'personal interest' items about military personnel and their families.

Although we cannot claim a precise validity, of the kind sought by opinion pollsters, for specific numerical findings, we do claim to establish significant relationships between religious affiliations and attitudes to the war. We should perhaps be more cautious in claiming representativeness for our sample of clergy, since rather less is known either about many social (and especially political)

110

characteristics of the clergy nationally, or about the specific features of the local clergy and the ways in which they differ from the national body. Nevertheless, by taking the whole population of our local clergy as our sample, we eliminated sampling errors, and although the response rate was lower than for the general population, the numbers of respondents were still sufficient to draw some conclusions.

In this chapter, we intend to discuss those of our findings which relate to religious attitudes in the general population, and to attitudes of clergy in particular. In our questionnaires, we asked people to identify themselves by religion; we did not (perhaps unfortunately - but the research was planned in a great hurry at the beginning of the war) ask our general sample more specific questions about religious involvement, e.g. about regularity of church attendance. The absence of this information is perhaps especially disabling when we consider Church of England identifiers, who constitute a large majority of the general sample, but there are nevertheless important differences between them and the Catholic, nonconformist and non-believing minorities which are revealed by our analysis.

Table 5.1
Breakdowns of samples by religious affiliation

	random sample	clergy
Church of England	68	55
Roman Catholic	8	9
other Christian	11	31
other religions	1	6
no religion	13	0
size of sample	1300	193
number of respondents	560	55
response rate	43	29

Table 5.1 compares our samples according to religious affiliation.[2] It will be seen that the numbers of members of non-Christian religions, both in the general sample and among the clergy, are too small to generate useful information. The number of Catholic priests (only five) is also too small a base from which to draw useful conclusions, so that although figures have been included so as to

111

make the data complete, they should be viewed with especial caution. The aggregration of 'other Christians' into a single group, while unfortunately obscuring differences between the smaller denominations, does at least enable us to engage in significant generalizations about both members and clergy in the nonconformist churches.

In the remainder of this paper, therefore, we shall present a four-way analysis between those who identify themselves as Anglicans, Roman Catholics, other Christians and belonging to no religion. We shall discuss the significant differences between those who identify with one of these four positions in general, and between ministers of the three Christian groupings. We shall discuss the ways in which the groups of clergy differ from their 'identifiers' in the general population, and from the general population as a whole. We shall be able to discuss the social characteristics of the religious groups in both the general sample and the clergy, and thus the ways in which differences of attitudes along religious lines may be related to other social and political factors.

Attitudes to the war

We asked our samples a number of questions designed to discover people's attitudes to the politics of the war, commencing with a question which had been asked by national opinion pollsters to establish the level of support (Table 5.2).[3] It will be seen that there was a lower level of approval of the war among clergy in general than among the population at large, but that this discrepancy existed only among Anglican and Catholic clergy (bearing in mind what we have said about the caution needed to interpret the figures for Catholic clergy). Among other, (principally nonconformist), Christians, the attitudes of ministers and ordinary members were very close.

This difference reflects an interesting paradox. Considering attitudes to the war in the population, approval is greater than average among Catholics (completely in disregard, it appears, of the Pope's position), and lower than average among nonconformists and (especially) those of no religion. Those who identify with the Church of England reflect (not surprisingly when one considers that they comprise over two-thirds of our sample) the average view of the population as a whole.

Considering attitudes to the war among the clergy, on the other hand, the Catholic clergy in our sample appear least pro-war,

Anglican clergy averagely pro-war (but still much less so than the general population), while nonconformist clergy are the most pro-war of all three groups. These patterns are maintained when we look at the answers to our next question, 'Do you think sanctions should have been given longer to work, before military force was used?' (Table 5.3). Clearly many - even more among the clergy than among the general population - who approved of Britain's involvement in the war, nevertheless still believed (in February 1991, on average about a month after the outbreak of war) that sanctions should have been given longer. This is perhaps a more interesting measure of underlying attitudes to the war than the simple question of approval or disapproval.[4]

Table 5.2
Approval/disapproval of British involvement in Gulf War

	strongly approve	approve	disapprove	strongly disapprove
Random sample (all)	28	52	10	7
Clergy (all denoms.)	16	51	11	19
Church of England				
population	30	55	8	6
clergy	14	55	14	17
Roman Catholic				
population	36	55	10	0
clergy	0	40	40	20
other Christians				
population	24	48	16	11
clergy	26	53	0	21
no religion				
population	22	46	22	10

Table 5.3
'Sanctions should have been given longer to work'

	agree	disagree
Random sample (all)	23	69
Clergy (all denoms.)	47	46
Church of England		
population	21	74
clergy	50	47
Roman Catholic		
population	21	69
clergy	80	0
other Christians		
population	37	60
clergy	37	58
no religion		
population	29	66

Once more, the nonconformist population are the least and their clergy the most pro-war, so that the discrepancy which exists between Anglican and Catholic clergy and their populations on the issue does not present itself among the nonconformists. It is interesting to speculate how far the relative pacifism of the nonconformists reflects the historic links of their traditions to peace causes (Martin, 1965). The lack of a split between clerical and lay attitudes in the nonconformist population, on the other hand, could reflect the fact that ministers are often elevated laymen.

We asked a number of questions designed to elucidate perceptions of the politics of the Gulf War. Respondents were allowed to choose up to two of the following statements as closest to their view of 'why Britain went to war':

'to get Iraq out of Kuwait',

'because we support the United Nations',

'to protect oil supplies',

'because we have to stand up to dictators',

and 'because we support America'.

114

As will be seen from Table 5.4, majorities of all groups identified with the manifest reason, to remove Iraq from Kuwait; but clergy were less likely than the general population to identify with the simple tabloid notion that 'we have to stand up to dictators', and more likely to agree with more cynical explanations to do with oil and supporting the USA. Once again, the congruence between popular and clerical views was greatest among nonconformists and weaker among Anglicans and Catholics. A similar pattern can be observed in views of Saddam Hussein (Table 5.5), where it can be seen that clergy are less likely to identify with the tabloid views of him as like Hitler or even mad.

Table 5.4
Reasons for war

	Iraq out of Kuwait	support UN	protect oil	stand up dictators	Support US
Random sample (all)	60	35	26	38	14
Clergy (all denoms.)	56	22	42	24	33
Church of England					
population	60	38	23	40	14
clergy	50	27	50	23	33
Roman Catholic					
population	67	33	26	43	2
clergy	40	20	60	0	60
other Christians					
population	70	27	25	39	16
clergy	70	30	25	30	25
no religion					
population	51	30	47	25	21

It might be expected, given Christian doctrines on war, that attitudes to killing would be differentiated more than attitudes to underlying political issues or personalities. This seems to be borne out by Table 5.6, which gives answers to choices between three views of violence in the war. Respondents were asked if they believed 'that nuclear weapons should be used to win the war against Iraq', 'that the minimum violence necessary should be used against Iraq to win the war', or 'that the violence of the war against Iraq cannot be justified'. It will be seen that there is minimal

Table 5.5
Perceptions of Saddam Hussein

	dangerous	like Hitler	mad	stands up for Arabs
Random sample (all)	82	35	23	4
Clergy (all denoms.)	86	18	7	7
Church of England				
population	81	40	24	3
clergy	93	17	3	7
Roman Catholic				
population	88	21	21	2
clergy	80	0	20	0
other Christians				
population	86	27	16	8
clergy	80	25	10	10
no religion				
population	80	25	21	1

support for the 'nuke them' position in the population (only among readers of the *Sun*, which had advocated this course, did support reach double figures - 21 per cent), and none among clergy. There was almost as little support in the general population for the view that the violence could not be justified - although more among nonconformists and non-believers than among Anglicans and Catholics. Among the clergy, however, this view was much more strongly subscribed to, again more among Anglicans and Catholics than among nonconformists. If one takes (although obviously many would not) pacifism as an indication of the influence of Christian beliefs, this would seem to indicate that they made a stronger difference to the attitudes of clergy than of ordinary believers, and indeed that non-believers were likelier to take a pacifist stance than Anglicans or Catholics. The difference between clerical and popular attitudes is underlined by replies to our question, 'How concerned are you about loss of life among the following groups of people?', in respect of Iraqi civilians and service personnel (Table 5.7). Here there are very large differences, with nearly half the general population, including most believers and non-believers, saying that they are 'not concerned' about loss of life among Iraqi service personnel. It should be stated that at the time

Table 5.6
Violence in the war

	use nuclear weapon	use minimum violence	violence not justified
Random sample (all)	6	81	5
Clergy (all denoms.)	0	69	27
Church of England			
population	7	82	5
clergy	0	67	27
Roman Catholic			
population	5	88	5
clergy	0	40	60
other Christians			
population	6	78	13
clergy	0	80	20
no religion			
population	4	73	13

Table 5.7
Concern for Iraqis

	Iraqi civilians			Iraqi service personnel		
	very conc.	conc.	not conc.	very conc.	conc.	not conc.
General sample (all)	42	43	16	26	30	44
Clergy (all denoms.)	87	13	0	69	24	4
Church of England						
population	42	42	16	26	29	45
clergy	87	13	0	62	31	7
Roman Catholic						
population	36	52	12	14	40	46
clergy	60	40	0	75	25	0
other Christians						
population	53	39	8	36	31	33
clergy	95	5	0	85	15	0
no religion	36	42	23	23	31	47

these questions were answered, this appeared a rather hypothetical questions, since no film had been shown and little reporting of Iraqi military casualties had been taken place in the British media. The evidence of mass slaughter, which emerged after coalition forces' attacks on the Iraqis retreating from Kuwait, and the gruesome estimates of up to 200,000 Iraqi casualties, were all still to come. The lack of concern should be taken more as a general indifference, rather than a specific callousness towards known killing. It is nevertheless quite striking as evidence of underlying attitudes.

This last point brings to our attention the fact that the war was, for most people in British society, entirely mediated by television. press and radio. Even those with relatives in the forces, who thanks to other modern media (such as the unprecedented facility to phone home from Saudi Arabia) were able to receive regular information from family members near the front, were not likely to obtain information very different from that provided by mass media. Indeed, family members of troops relied on television for information.

The mass media were able to report, for the most part, only what the coalition and Iraqi authorities wanted or allowed them to see. During most of the war there was a remarkably successful control of information, which meant that few if any bodies were seen in either film or still photographs in the media.[5] In addition to this, of course, some British newspapers actively promoted luridly patriotic views of the war, and demonized Saddam Hussein in ways which are reflected in the perceptions of him (especially as being 'mad' or 'like Hitler') revealed in Table 5.5, above.

In order to gauge attitudes to the media, we asked our respondents a number of questions about television and the national and local press. In particular we asked whether each of these 'glorified the war too much', had 'a sensible attitude to the war', or was 'too critical of the war'. Readers of tabloid newspapers, although (as replies to other questions showed) clearly influenced by their newspapers' attitudes, were more likely than those of quality papers to see their papers as 'glorifying the war too much'. Television was also seen as 'glorifying the war too much' by 40 per cent of those who replied *before* 13 February (when both BBC and ITV showed extensive film of the Baghdad bunker in which several hundred civilians died); only 2 per cent, at this stage, saw television coverage as 'too critical' of the war.

The bunker bombing was clearly a major departure in television coverage of the war, and we found that attitudes shifted among those who replied after this incident: fewer (but still nearly 30 per cent) thought that coverage was glorifying the war, while the minority judging coverage too critical grew (but remained under 10 per cent of the sample). (Even among Conservative supporters in our sample, who might have been expected to be influenced by Conservative MPs' criticisms of television news, the minority seeing television as over-glorifying war was greater than that finding it too critical.)

As Table 5.8 shows, among the general population, Catholics were significantly less like to see television as 'glorifying the war too much' than Anglicans or, especially, nonconformists and non-believers. The clergy were, generally, more likely than the general population to see television coverage in this light.

Finally, we asked all our respondents, 'have you been affected personally by the war in one of the following ways?', and specified 'feeling worried about family members or friends in the Gulf', 'feeling good because of British or allied successes' or 'feeling worried by the violence of the war in general'; we also offered the option of stating that they hadn't been affected personally by the war. As can be seen from Table 5.9, clergy were more likely to say that they were 'worried in general' by the war, and less likely to say that they 'felt good' about allied successes or were not affected.

Table 5.8
Attitudes to television coverage

	glorifies war too much	sensible attitude	too critical of war
Random sample (all)	29	59	13
Clergy (all denoms.)	35	46	2
Church of England			
population	32	59	9
clergy	42	54	4
Roman Catholic			
population	22	69	9
clergy	100	0	0
other Christians			
population	38	55	7
clergy	25	75	0
no religion	38	53	8

Table 5.9

Ways in which people were personally affected by the war

	worried/ family etc	feel good	worried/ general	not affected
General sample (all)	13	12	35	40
Clergy (all denoms.)	15	7	51	22
Church of England				
population	12	12	32	43
clergy	15	4	63	19
Roman Catholic				
population	19	14	31	36
clergy	40	40	20	0
other Christians				
population	11	8	46	35
clergy	10	10	50	30
no religion	12	13	39	34

Surprisingly, given that the clergy reported many fewer family connections with people in the Gulf than did the general population, they were as likely to claim to be 'worried about family or friends'; one might guess that they were likely to be concerned about parishioners involved in the Gulf.

Explanations for differences in attitudes in the general population

Our analysis has established a very clear pattern of differences in attitudes, between members of different religions, and between members of the general population and of the clergy. In the random sample of the general population, those who identified themselves as Catholics were more likely to be pro-war, less likely to want sanctions to have been given longer, less likely to endorse 'cynical' reasons for the war, less likely to believe the violence of the war unjustified, less likely to be concerned about loss of life among Iraqis, and less likely to see television as glorifying the war, than were members of other religious groups or none. They were, in short, consistently the most pro-war or least pacifist group in the general population. At the other extreme, nonconformists and non-believers were almost equally consistently the least pro-war or most pacifistic groups. This spectrum of positions, with Catholics at one extreme, nonconformists and non-believers at the other, and Anglican identifiers in a middle position, holds remarkably well for most issues. Only when it comes to perceptions, rather than attitudes, does the pattern break; Catholics are less likely than any other group to endorse the descriptions of Saddam Hussein as 'mad' or 'like Hitler'. The fact that their attitudes to the war are irrespective of specific perceptions only makes the differences more intriguing.

The attitudes of the Catholics are, of course, all the more interesting because their spiritual leader, the Pope, had taken a clear position against the war. It might be thought that British Catholics were ignorant of the Pope's position, but in our second survey we asked respondents to say which, of a number of political and religious figures, had been 'for' or 'against' the war. The replies we received suggest, as Table 5.10 shows, that the Pope's position was widely understood, unlike the Archbishop of Canterbury's, whose ambiguity tended to make more anti-war respondents see him as anti-war. British Catholic leaders may have taken less uncompromising positions than the Pope's, of course, but is still necessary to explain why Catholics should be the least pacifistic group.

The differences in attitudes which we have found between members of different denominations and none are not enormous, of course, and it is possible that they could be explained by other social differences between the religious groupings in the population. It is not obvious, however, what these differences could be. In the course of our wider study, we found that factors such as age, sex, class and voting intention did have modest influences of various aspects of people's attitudes to the war. The most marked differences, however, were those between readers of different kinds of newspapers, with readers of the *Sun* and *Star* - the most downmarket, jingoistic tabloids - most strongly pro-war, and readers of quality newspapers the most likely to take a pacfistic line, with readers of the *Mirror* and the middle-market Conservative tabloids taking positions in between.[7]

When we examine our main sample in terms of newspaper readership, we find that there are no obvious correlations between the differences of newspaper readership between the denominations, and the differences of attitudes towards the Gulf War (Table 5.11). The Catholics in our sample, the most pro-war group, are less likely to read tabloid newspapers as a whole than are

Table 5.10
Perceptions of religious leaders' views on the war

	Pope	Archbishop Runcie
For war	4	30
Against war	74	48

Church of England identifiers; while the nonconformist and non-believing groups, on the whole the least pro-war, have radically different newspaper-reading profiles. The nonconformists tend to read Conservative tabloid newspapers, with few reading the *Mirror* or the *Guardian*; and they also include more readers of the Conservative *Yorkshire Post* than any other denomination. The nonbelievers, on the other hand, include the smallest proportion of readers of Conservative tabloids (both down- and mid-market) and large proportions of *Mirror* and (especially) *Guardian* readers. Merely on the basis of newspaper readership, we could predict no difference in attitudes to the war between Catholics and nonconformists (or if anything, one which went in the opposite direction to that which we actually found); and we would predict that the nonconformists would be more pro-war than the non-believers (whereas if anything, it is the other way).

Table 5.11
Newspapers read by religious identifiers in general population

	C of E	RC	other Christian	no religion
Sun/Star readers	16	14	15	12
Mirror readers	16	11	5	16
other tabloid readers	26	17	20	15
Guardian readers	1	3	2	15
other quality readers	5	8	9	10
Yorkshire Post readers	3	3	7	2
no daily morning paper	35	45	43	31

What this would tend to suggest is that religion did make a difference to attitudes to the war among the general population, irrespective of other influences. There may be something about the culture of nonconformist Christianity which means that beliefs have a much more practical impact on its adherents' attitudes than do those of other forms of Christianity; whereas for Catholics and Anglicans, this is less so. It is also important to consider here the divergence between clerical and popular attitudes among both Anglicans and (tentatively, given the numbers in our sample) Catholics; this suggests beliefs which have a different meaning for priests than for people.

The relation of non-belief to attitudes also needs to be explored here. Clearly non-adherence to a religion hardly constitutes as coherent an ideological position as adherence to even a broad Christian grouping such as is represented by our 'other Christian' category. 'No religion' is a residual, negative statement; non-religious people are not necessarily 'non-believers' in a broader sense - they may believe in a variety of values or ideologies. Interestingly, although taken as a whole they are less pro-war (Table 5.2) than any group of Christians, they are no more like to believe in giving sanctions longer (Table 5.3) and *more* likely to say they are 'not concerned' about Iraqi civilians (Table 5.7). This last point, especially, is interesting, since it suggests that the non-believers may be more heterogeneous than the Christian groups, containing, at one pole, a caring humanistic (stereotypically *Guardian*-reading) group, and at the other an uncaring, nihilistic (*Sun*-reading?) group.

Explanations for attitudes among the clergy

As we have seen in Tables 5.1-5.10, attitudes to the war among clergy differed between denominations; whereas the nonconformist clergy had very similar attitudes to the nonconformist population (both being less pro-war than the population as a whole), the Anglican and (tentatively) the Catholic clergy were less pro-war still than the nonconformist clergy, and even less pro-war compared to Anglicans and Catholics in the population. Taking the clergy as a whole, therefore, what were the reasons why they were much less pro-war than the general population?

We took special care to analyse the characteristics of our clerical sample, in order to explain these divergences. The clergy are, of course, by definition a professional 'middle-class' grouping, where the population as a whole contain a large majority of 'working class' and non-professional 'middle-class' groups. In addition, as can be seen from Table 5.12, the clergy in our sample tended to be overwhelmingly more male and older than the general population; they are far less likely to read a tabloid newspaper or, indeed, the local newspaper (an interesting comment itself on their awareness of the local community); they are far less likely, given their age and sex, to have seen any form of military service[8] or to have family connections with the military; and they are (slightly) less likely to vote Conservative.

Table 5.12
Characteristics of clergy, compared to general population

	fem	u 45	reads: tab- loid	reads: local paper	services: self	services: family	votes: C	votes: Lab	votes: LD
General sample	51	52	53	72	18	22	27	28	13
Clergy (all)	5	27	7	27	18	5	20	26	16

The clergy are, therefore, a social group distinguished quite sharply in social and ideological terms from the wider community of which they are a part. We may speculate that the nonconformist ministry, including many lay ministers, is less socially distant from its church membership. Conversely we might argue that nonconformity is a more active religious identification for members of the population than either Catholicism, which is very much a matter of birth and family, or Anglicanism, which is in many cases a highly residual, formal identification.

If therefore we are to suggest that 'religion' has an influence on attitudes, it is not so much religion considered narrowly as beliefs or doctrine, but religion considered as a culture or sub-culture with varying degrees of active participation by its members. We would obviously expect this to be stronger in the case of ministers, whose whole lives are bound up with religion, than of ordinary church members, still less members of the general population whose identification with a religion may be historical, formal or residual rather than active.

Nevertheless, if clergy do adopt distinctive attitudes, this may be not merely because of their religious beliefs considered in isolation, but because of the way these relate to other aspects of their experience and belief systems. We found that several factors, in addition to denomination, differentiated attitudes among the clergy who responded to our survey. Age made some difference: while younger and older ministers were equally likely to approve or disapprove of the war, a clear majority of younger ministers thought sanctions should have been given longer, while a majority of older ministers disagreed with this.

Age was related to newspaper readership. All but one of the younger ministers read the *Guardian, Independent* or *Times*; while 70 per cent of older ministers read these papers, 30 per cent of them read the *Telegraph, Yorkshire Post* or a tabloid. There were no *Sun* or *Star* readers among the clergy, and the few tabloid readers were not a large enough number from which to draw hard and fast conclusions. Nevertheless, all the tabloid readers among clergy approved of the war and thought that sanctions should not have been given longer; none of them were among those who believed that the violence of the war could not be justified; none of them thought television had glorified the war too much; and all them agreed that their papers were 'patriotic' rather than 'too patriotic' (which most of the quality readers saw their papers as).

Another age-related factor which we investigated was military experience. In our study as a whole we found that military experience or connections correlated to a modest, but significant degree with attitudes to the war (only 10 per cent of those with such links were anti-war, compared to 20 per cent in the rest of the population) (Shaw and Carr-Hill, 1991b). Among the clergy. only a small minority (less than a fifth) had military experience themselves, and only a tiny number had family connections. The majority of older clergy were unusual, in their generation, in having escaped military service. It was interesting, therefore, to note that there were significant differences in attitudes to the war between clergy with personal military experience, and those without (Table 5.13). The former are generally more pro-war

Table 5.13
Military participation and attitudes to the war among clergy

	military participation	no participation
disapprove of war	15	35
sanctions should be given longer	31	54
violence of war not justified	23	29
'very concerned' about Iraqi servicemen	61	75
television glorifies war too much	36	44
television too informative	54	16

(although interestingly almost as likely to say that sanctions should have been given longer); they are also more likely to say that television coverage was over-informative. An even clearer differentiator of clerical attitudes is voting intention. As will be seen from Table 5.14, there is a veritable gulf in attitudes between anti-war Labour- and pro-war Conservative-voting ministers (with Liberal Democrat ministers in a middle position, but closer to their Labour-voting colleagues). Both the ministers who said they were 'not concerned' about the loss of Iraqi servicemen's lives were intending to vote Conservative.

Table 5.14
Voting intention and attitudes to the war among clergy

	Con	Lab	LD
disapprove of war	0	57	42
sanctions should be given longer	27	93	39
violence of war not justified	0	57	31
'very concerned' about Iraqi servicemen	55	75	77
television glorifies war too much	20	67	55
television too informative	30	8	25

There was also an interesting correlation between party identification and military links: 30 per cent of those without experience of the Second World War or National Service supported Labour, but none of those with military experience did. Similarly 30 per cent of those without family connections with those directly involved in the Gulf conflict voted Labour, but none of those with such connections did. Taking those without any sort of military connections, 31 per cent voted Labour; of those with, 8 per cent did.

What these findings suggest is not necessarily that relation to the military or voting intention as such, rather than religious belief, actually determined attitudes to the war among the clergy. But they do imply that if, as our denominational findings imply, religious beliefs have a bearing on attitudes to war, then other social factors are relevant to how religious beliefs are actually interpreted. Military experience and links may tend to incline ministers to be both Conservative and pro-war. Equally, those who interpret their Christian beliefs in an anti-war direction also tend to interpret them as implying Labour, or at least Liberal Democrat, rather than Conservative politics.

These findings are important for the overall interpretation of the role of religion in determining attitudes to war. Clearly religious beliefs are not held in isolation from social experience, culture or secular political values. If religious beliefs - or for that matter a rejection of them - play a part in determining attitudes, this is because religious ideas are one way, articulated with others, of actively expressing a relationship with the world. The world, in this context, is the complex of social relationships in which people are involved.

Conclusion

Social surveys can only give certain snapshots of people's opinions at given points in time; they also depend a lot on the questions asked. What our surveys suggest is that members of the general population, and even more ministers of religion, were influenced in their attitudes to the Gulf War by their religious identifications and beliefs. Nevertheless, it is clear that they were influenced by other factors; much of our discussion has centred on relatively modest variations in attitudes. On the basic issue of approval of the war, we found 17 per cent of the population as a whole dissenting, but 27 per cent of nonconformist Christians and 32 per cent of those who claimed no religion. Likewise, no more than 30 per cent of ministers of religion dissented from this position. If religion accounts for these variations, there is still to be considered the basic fact that a large majority of clergy, and an even larger majority of all religious adherents in the general population, supported the war.

Our research cannot tell us whether this stance of the majority was right or wrong, nor can it tell us what part religious beliefs played in justifying it. Our analyses do show us that a range of factors, including age, sex, class, military participation and party identification, also played a part in determining variations in attitudes, and that newspaper readership was a more powerful factor than all of these. How precisely religious beliefs related to these other elements in determining people's attitudes is perhaps a question which survey analysis can pose but cannot fully answer. Other sorts of research are necessary to complement our findings and take these questions further.

Notes

1. The influence of memory is discussed in Shaw, 1994.
2. In this and subsequent tables, figures are given as percentages except where otherwise indicated.
3. In this and subsequent tables, 'don't knows' and non-responses have not been represented, but since figures have not been adjusted to exclude them, it is possible for the reader to calculate the proportion of respondents who did not choose one of the answers given.
4. The discrepancy between the views of the clergy and of the general population on this issue was probably even greater than these figures suggest. The average date of returning the questionnaire was earlier for the general population than for the clergy, but we found that retrospective support for sanctions was - understandably in the circumstances - a declining cause, the longer the war continued.
5. The control of information in the war is discussed in Taylor.
6. Figures given for the random sample as a whole are for responses *after* 13 February (in order to make them comparable to clergy, all of whom replied after this date). Figures for religious groups in the population include, however, responses before 13 February, and so overstate the tendency of these groups to see television coverage as over-glorifying, in comparison with the relevant groups of clergy.
7. This is examined more fully in Shaw and Carr-Hill, 1991a.
8. Only 18 per cent of clergy reported they themselves had full-time military experience; in all cases this dated from the Second World War or National Service. Considering that over two-thirds of the clergy were of an age to have served in either the war or National Service, this is a low figure; if ministers were typical of their age and sex, the figure would probably be about 60 per cent. Only one minister reported involvement with the Territorials. No clergy reported family involvement in the Gulf.

References

Martin, D. (1965), *Pacifism*, Routledge and Kegan Paul, London.
Mowlana, H., Gerbner, G.W. and Schiller, H. (eds.) (1992), *Triumph of the Image: The Media's War in the Persian Gulf. A Global Perspective*, Westview Press, Boulder, Colorado.

Shaw, M. (1991), *Post-Military Society Militarism, Demilitarization and War at the end of the Twentieth Century*, Polity, Cambridge.

Shaw, M. (1994), 'Past Wars and Present Conflicts: From the Second World War to the Gulf', paper presented at Conference on War and Memory, Portsmouth (Publication forthcoming in Lunn, K. and Evans, M., *War and Memory*.

Shaw, M. (1995, forthcoming), *Distant Violence: Media and Civil Society in the New Global Crises*, Pinter, London.

Shaw, M. and Carr-Hill, R. (1991a), 'Mass Media and Attitudes to the Gulf War in Britain', *Electronic Journal of Communication/Revue Electronique de Communication*, special issue.

Shaw, M. and Carr-Hill, R. (1991b), *Public Opinion, Media and Violence: Attitudes to the Gulf War in a Local Population*, Hull University Gulf War Project, Hull.

Shaw, M. and Carr-Hill, R. (1992), 'Public Opinion and Media War Coverage in Britain', in Mowlana et al. (eds.), pp. 144-157.

Taylor, P.M. (1992), *War and the Media: Propaganda and Persuasion in the Gulf War*, Manchester University Press, Manchester.

Index

References from Notes and Bibliographies are indicated by 'n' after page reference.

131

132

DATE DUE

			Printed in USA